D1316201

My BLIND DATE went BLIND!

True Stories of Dates Gone Wrong*

*Plus a few happy endings

BY VIRGINIA VITZTHUM

Workman Publishing • New York

Copyright © 2010 by Virginia Vitzthum

Interior illustrations copyright © 2010 by Lou Brooks c/o theispot.com

Library of Congress Cataloging-in-Publication Data

Vitzthum, Virginia.
  My blind date went blind : --and other crazy true stories of dates gone
wrong / by Virginia Vitzthum.
      p. cm.
  ISBN 978-0-7611-5541-6 (alk. paper)
  1. Dating (Social customs)--Humor. 2. Blind dates--Humor.
3. Online dating--Humor. I. Title.
  HQ801.V63 2010
  306.73082--dc22

                              2010002639

Workman books are available at special discounts when purchased in
bulk for premiums and sales promotions as well as for fund-raising or
educational use. Special editions of book excerpts can also be created
to specification. For details, contact the Special Sales Director at the
address below or send an e-mail to specialsales@workman.com.

Design by Rae Ann Spitzenberger
Cover illustration by Lou Brooks
Author photo by Lizzie Himmel

Grateful acknowledgment is made for permission to reprint poem page vi,
copyright © 2008 by Cody Walker from *Shuffle and Breakdown* by
Cody Walker, by permission of The Waywiser Press.

WORKMAN PUBLISHING COMPANY, INC.
225 Varick Street
New York, NY 10014-4381
www.workman.com

Printed in the United States of America
First printing March 2010
10 9 8 7 6 5 4 3 2 1

Contents

Blind Date
A poem

I'm sorry but
I can't see you anymore.

—*Cody Walker*

Introduction

What Could Go Wrong?

"YOU'LL LOVE HIM," SAYS THE FRIEND. "She's great!" says the coworker. "I'm romantic, kind, successful, funny, fit, creative, fun, and looking for someone to pamper!" scream the pixels on your computer screen.

In the face of all this hype, no matter how many bad dates we've had, how are we supposed to keep our hopes down?

Any available detail is used to stoke the fire. I can't believe that's her favorite book too. His "What I'm Looking For" is me! Everyone else I've dated thought my trainspotting hobby was weird, but he does it every weekend—what are the odds? Before we know it, "blind" has been eclipsed by "date" and we've started singing while we dress.

We meet for our drink or our coffee. And usually, we fall from the cliff of hope, legs a spinning blur, into the bad-date abyss. We were sure this time the Acme rocket would shoot straight. That the bomb wouldn't blow up in our face. That this time, we'd catch that Road Runner. How, like Wile E. Coyote, did we get fooled again?

If a friend was to blame for the encounter that left our fur singed and our eyeballs hanging to the ground, we wonder, What on earth was this yenta-friend *thinking*? But she (usually she) tried, and we owe it to her not to blame or question. Though how can we refrain from wondering whether she truly considers us as big a loser as our date seems to warrant? At least when the computer sets you up with a dud, you needn't try to read the tea leaves. You were just the victim of a crappy algorithm.

> We fall from the cliff of hope, legs a spinning blur, into the bad-date abyss.

Let's face it: Meeting a stranger with the hope of a romantic partnership is a setup for slapstick, which is why most of the stories in this book are amusing disasters. There are, however, a handful of happy endings. They feature the same false assumptions, faux pas, and missed signals as the dates gone wrong. (Because where's the fun in a smooth, "we just knew" date?)

So what did the happy-enders do differently?

They had luck and timing on their side, sure, but they also hung in there a little longer. They resisted the temptation to make the whole date a cartoonish anecdote at the first malfunction. They let the person, the situation, the relationship deepen into three dimensions. They relaxed their pursuit and extended some empathy. A bunch of bad dates can make anyone *feel* like Wile E., Elmer Fudd, or poor, sweet Betty, always a step behind Veronica in the Archie hunt. But in real life there are other endings. And we get to write them.

Or, in the case of this book, I get to write them. These stories were all told or sent to me, but I have changed names (except where noted) and identifying details. The stories in first person are not transcripts; but I tried to be faithful to the daters' voices.

DREAMS
(and Nightmares)

On a dream date, you feel like you've traveled to another country—one in which there's no need for convention. You're not graded on timeliness or minor breaches of etiquette; you're dancing an effortless dance of laughter and attraction. Your country of two needs no laws (and that's part of what makes it so exciting).

On a nightmare date, you realize how very much you do need those rules. In the absence of connection, a disregard for convention can be scary. When you realize that this stranger is not following any social mores at all, you wonder what exactly he is capable of. Unfairly, the same utterance—"Our kids would be so cute"—can be charming on a dream date and creepy on a nightmare date. Just like the most memorable dreams, it makes little sense.

The Lesson

The date as learning opportunity
Joyce M., 28

YES, HE DESCRIBED HIMSELF in his online profile as "a lawyer resembling Eminem," but I hadn't had a date in a while. I decided to accept his invitation to meet after work at a vodka bar in downtown Manhattan.

He was on the corner stool in conversation with the bartender, looking like a regular. And he did look like Eminem—pale, scrawny, pouting—but an Eminem who gelled his hair too much and wore tortoiseshell glasses that inadvertently made him look young, rather than sophisticated. He didn't even look like he shaved.

He greeted me with a nervous backslap and insisted I order a martini made with ginger-infused vodka. "Trust me, I drink here every night, a lot. I know what's good." He was like a child who'd learned to play a man by watching 1950s movies.

The drink was good (the bartender gave me the

recipe, so one good thing came from the evening). Em poured his own drink down the hatch and proceeded to talk nonstop about himself. He knew my first name and found out nothing else over the next hour and a half.

He was a personal injury attorney at Johnnie Cochran's law firm—and boy was he proud of his work. He went on and *on* about all the good the firm did for children and the infirm. Some memorable utterances: "Did you know lead paint tastes like candy? You didn't know that, did you?" And "Johnnie Cochran is a saint. Someday people will recognize that." (This was in 2003, before Cochran passed away.)

After maybe an hour of this monologue, I went to the bathroom and plotted my escape. I would ask for the check. That can usually deflate a puffed-up man—you steal their moves and they don't know what to do. Game over.

As I walked back, Eminem looked me up and down with a smile that wasn't friendly. I firmly gestured to the bartender. Eminem smirked. "A modern woman, eh? Pay your own way? You can take care of yourself, is that it?"

What a strange, oily, sexist young curmudgeon. Was he Eminem or was he Spencer Tracy?

I ignored him and reached into my purse. But I couldn't find my wallet. I kept calm, made it a joke at first. "Okay, my wallet has to be somewhere," I said briskly while I pawed the contents of my purse again.

"You left your purse here when you went to the bathroom?"

"Yes, why, did you see something?" I hated him so much I couldn't bear to look at him.

"No, but that wasn't very smart, was it?"

Now I looked at him, and I raised my voice. "What is your problem? Why don't you help me look?!" The bartender and a few people at the bar glanced over. I was close to yelling. He continued to smirk. I patted my coat pockets and dug through my purse a fifth time. I ran back into the bathroom and scanned the stalls. Fuck. Credit cards, license, expense report receipts, seventy-three dollars in cash, fuck, fuck, fuck.

I headed back to the bar, where ambulance-chasing Slim Shady was still grinning evilly at me. My teeth gritted. "Hey, calm down," he commanded, the smile still in his voice.

I breathed in and out. "Look, it's probably better if you either help look or don't talk to me."

"Listen, Joyce. Look at me."

"What?!" I growled, spinning to look at him, "What do you—" I stopped. He was holding my wallet out, long-suffering patience in his eyes.

"I took it to teach you a lesson. You shouldn't trust people so much."

I used the wallet to knock his ginger martini into his lap. The two women sitting next to us applauded as I strode outside, where I counted my money.

The Little Revolutionary

Trippy, but the wrong kind . . .

Sarah D.,* 58

(*RELEVANT NAME *NOT* CHANGED)

IT WAS THE LATE 1960S, but you'd never have known it at my boarding school in Massachusetts. Only girls matriculated there, with boys allowed in just two buildings on campus, neither of them dorms.

The boys who did make it through our stone gates did not have long hair or wear T-shirts with slogans; we greeted them in dresses worn over stockings held up by industrial white garter belts. They came every few weeks for heavily chaperoned dances or lectures or films.

I lagged behind even in these frozen times. In my junior year, my only extracurricular activity was serving as president of the T. S. Eliot club, run by a storklike teacher whose prize possession was an actual letter from the great poet. We'd take the letter out and look at it—no touching!—at the end of every meeting.

I had never had a date or kissed a boy. I was five feet eleven inches tall, stooped to concavity, myopic. I call Miss Harrington storklike in sisterhood if not envy, as I looked like an even spindlier version of that *Ciconiidae* genus, so graceful when airborne, and so gawky when earthbound in cat-eye glasses and a plaid shift from the Tall Girls Shop.

My roommate Nan was much more worldly than I. She had already dated and kissed several boys, and she was determined to have me join the ranks of the kissed. Her brother, Chip, went to our male counterpart boarding school in the next town. She convinced him to arrange a date for me by agreeing to write his civics paper on the Communist threat. I refused to go alone, so she and Chip agreed to "double-date" with us.

After dinner, Nan came over to my room to groom me for my debut. She forced me to wear a tight sweater of hers. Four inches of pale arm stretched skeletally past the cuffs. I sat on the bed and turned my blind eyes up to her for makeup, wresting back my glasses when she tried to keep them. "Your eyes are your best feature, and you just hide them," she wailed, but admitted she didn't want to lead me around like a German shepherd during the rendezvous.

We walked to the dining hall, where we boarded the school bus to the gym at St. Joe's with about fifteen other girls. The boys' school was showing *Guess Who's Coming to Dinner,* a movie considered quite daring around our campus.

It was May, one of the first warm nights. The girls piled out of the bus into male territory, chattering and preening. It was exciting. I felt I was being admitted into normal adult life—an exotic mystery at the time.

"There he is," Nan said, squeezing my arm. We walked over to Chip and a very short fellow in a seersucker suit. The short boy held a thick cane with an ornate carved handle. My eyes drifted sympathetically down to his feet and legs to see if he was crippled.

He looked at Nan with hopeful eyebrows, then at me in panic. He was easily six inches shorter than I was. I tried to telescope my neck down into my spine. Chip picked all this up. "Willie, let me present my sister, Nan, who has a boyfriend, and her friend Sarah, who does not. Girls, this is Willie Wolfe."

> The short boy held a thick cane with an ornate carved handle.

"Enchanté," said Willie, bending low to kiss Nan's hand, then mine. He twirled his hand in front of his forehead as he came up. "At your service, ladies." He moved the cane around in his hands, trying for a dandy effect, but seeming more like a majorette. Nan and I exchanged glances, and Chip led us into the gym. Willie walked fine; I could not figure out what the cane was for.

We picked a row of gray folding chairs and filed in: Chip, Nan, me, then Willie on the aisle. I had no idea how to talk to this affected creature, so I didn't. I turned on my chair and murmured to Nan.

Almost immediately there was a shout and a thud from the aisle. I swiveled around and saw a boy sprawled on the ground. He rolled onto his back and glared at Willie.

"What'd ya do that for?" he demanded.

"Do what?" Willie said slyly, twirling the cane between his knees.

"Trip me, you ass!"

"I'm sure your clumsiness is none of my affair," Willie purred. He turned to me and continued, "You must excuse the gracelessness of my classmates, Sally."

"Sarah," I said, shrinking away from him. I kept looking forward, around the room at the other students, and this time I saw him do it: He stuck his cane out in the aisle as a boy approached, tripped him, then pulled the cane back before anyone else could see! Then he turned to me and started talking like Tennessee Williams again.

I whispered to Nan, "There's something wrong with him! He's tripping people with that pretentious cane. Can I leave?"

"There's no way to get back to school till the bus comes back, after the movie. I think we're stuck," Nan hissed back. To her credit, she then turned to Chip and started whispering furiously at him. (He later explained that he thought Willie and I "both liked books.")

I sat there in misery for the next two hours. Willie tripped six more people with his cane before, during, and after the movie. On the bus home, I raged at Nan and she sympathized, said she'd given Chip a piece of both our minds. Also stirred by the movie, I implored Nan, "How could anyone object to a nice Negro like Sidney Poitier when lunatics like Willie roam free?" I began to fret that starting my dating life with a sadistic, foppish dwarf might set a tone.

Thankfully it did not. In fact I'm quite sure Willie Wolfe is the craziest person I ever dated. I never saw him in person again, but six years later, there he was all over my television and the newspapers. Willie Wolfe, a.k.a. Cujo, had gone West from boarding school to become a member of the Symbionese Liberation Army and kidnapper of Patty Hearst. In May 1974 he died in a fiery shootout with the Los Angeles police's S.W.A.T. team.

BLIND DATE OFFENSE #43
Bringing a weapon

The Emperor's New Clothes

A young newcomer sees New York naked

Maria R., 27

IT WAS THE SUMMER OF 2004, and I had lived in New York less than a year. The city was socially tougher than I'd expected.

I'd moved from a small town in Tennessee with no men, and figured that a city with millions of people would solve all my problems. But instead, I had a sort of second adolescence. It took me an embarrassing number of tries to figure out that the charming fellow with whom I'd had the nice evening and great sex didn't actually want to be my boyfriend now.

I spent a lot of time on Friendster that first year. My friends and I used it as the social networking tool it was intended to be—I built upon my friendships back home to meet new people in New York—but we also used it as a dating site, searching for people in our age range and area.

In June, I got a Friendster message from a reasonably attractive guy with a shaved head, angular glasses, and a kind of knowing, lopsided smile. He asked what kind of writing I did and we corresponded back and forth a couple times. He invited me to a writing group held at a Midtown bookstore that was owned by someone in his family. It all seemed very civilized, with a hint of potential romance.

I wore a black sweater and a modest skirt with fishnets—artsy, cute, not too slutty. To read, I brought a satirical short story about a yuppie couple trying to adopt a boy-sized grub. It was an absurdist send-up of the trend of cross-cultural adoption.

At the bookstore, I immediately recognized Tyler from his Friendster photo. He greeted me warmly and ushered me upstairs with a hand on my lower back. Perfectly gentlemanly. Tyler seemed very old-school New York. A baseball-loving, over-intellectualizing, Upper West Side Woody Allen type with very little muscle tone and lots of connections.

And the bookstore—what a place! It made me feel nostalgic for something I'd never really experienced. The musty smell of leather-bound first editions, antique globes from Colonial times, the rolling ladder— Tyler was made much cuter by the bookstore.

The second story (philosophy, history, poetry) was

packed with attractive women in their twenties and a few nerdy guys. It seemed as if Tyler had been scouring the city for women to invite to this event where he would be in charge, in his element, showing off his talent. I had known intellectually that I probably wasn't the only woman he'd Friendster-flirted with, but my heart quailed even as I laughed at his chutzpah.

I was still intimidated by everything New York. I reeled a couple times a week at how much stuff in the city I recognized from TV, movies, songs, and books. The screaming fights between cabdriver and pedestrian and the tirades at some unspecified "motherfucker" by foul-smelling lunatics on the subway still rattled me. Everyone else seemed blasé, even amused. It was a big deal for me to bring my earnest short story to read in front of that group.

People stood up and read from their typed pages, and then everyone else discussed the stories. The women, uniformly cute, were not great writers and neither were the nerdy guys or Tyler. The criticism was not at a very high level either. Everyone seemed nice enough, just not as skilled as I'd expected. My story was plenty good! My chest puffed up a little—I could hold my own among these pretenders! But they ran out of time before I could read.

As the bookstore was closing, Tyler called out an invite—back to his place to continue reading! About eight women and four men took the bait. First we all had dinner together at a noodle house, which was great. We were all strangers to one another, so I wasn't the new person for a change, and we chattered on about writing. (I was getting better at the insincere "enjoyed that" or "great!" with every reading/music gig/art opening/play I went to.)

At dinner, Tyler told me about his family and the book he was working on—something about baseball that he seemed casually certain would be published within a year or two.

The screaming fights between cabdriver and pedestrian, the tirades by foul-smelling lunatics on the subway . . .

Then we all followed him across the park to his apartment on the Upper West Side. When he opened the door, I saw a mosaic of colors and images. As the twelve of us filed into the tiny, spotless studio—there was only room for a bed and a desk—a wave of silence swept through the little group.

There were naked people all around us. There were magazine pages of bodies pasted on every wall from floor to ceiling. Some of the images were mild, like Kate Moss in a see-through top. Others were pornographic: An erect penis peeked out from behind a curtain. For a minute we all kind of quietly gawked. We hadn't been warned.

Tyler seemed to enjoy his guests' surprise. It almost felt like a test. One beat of silence passed, then two, then everyone started murmuring pleasantries. "Oh, wow. How long did it take you to do this?" "Is that Madonna?" "Hey, that's from a perfume ad. I have that perfume." No one really seemed shocked. I sneaked looks at their faces. Nobody else seemed to think it was antifeminist or pathetic or sort of aggressive.

"This is where you write your baseball book?" was my stab at humor and it sounded prudish. Everybody laughed, so I did, too. The others found spots on his bed to sit and discuss, while I sat on the floor with some other woman who I don't remember at all. (I was completely distracted by all the boobs, butts, and penises on display.) I calculated how long I needed to hang out to officially *not* be leaving in a snit, made my apologies, and took off.

I couldn't imagine sharing my story in that room. I didn't even like talking to people in that room. I tripped down the steps to the sidewalk. Everybody outside was dressed; even some dogs were wearing T-shirts. I took a big, happy breath and wondered how long the others would sit in that tiny room pretending not to look at the walls.

BLIND DATE OFFENSE #57
Oversharing

Over the Borderline (Personality)

Do vegans eat dessert?

Sandy S., 35

IT WAS A HALF-BLIND DATE: Rafe had seen me with my friend David in the park and asked about me. David told me he didn't know Rafe well, but that he seemed very intelligent and unique. "He marches to the beat of his own drummer," he said. I was flattered, and I was lonely. I told David to give the guy my number.

It took Rafe a month to call me, and he didn't refer to the time elapsed. "My friend is having an art opening," he said. "I think you should see his work. Then I'll take you to dinner."

He told me he'd wear a beret so I'd know it was him. "Oh, no, really, you don't have to do that," I demurred. "Just tell me what color shirt you're wearing." But he insisted. Ugh. It was hard to miss him when I got there, the middle-aged guy who looked like a cartoon of an artist. I'd hoped he might take it off once I'd found him, but no. He wore it all night.

As we walked to dinner, he blurted out, "My stepfather was a murderer." I waited for him to go on but he was silent.

What do you say to that? What I came up with was, "Who did he kill?"

The vegan restaurant did not serve any alcohol.

Instead of answering, Rafe said, "Where do you want to eat? What do you like?" Hmm. My appetite had disappeared and I knew I wanted this date to end quickly, so I pointed to the nearest restaurant and said, "This one here looks great."

"No, we can't go there, I'm vegan."

"Fine. You decide then."

The vegan restaurant did not serve any alcohol, so I sat through the ensuing dinner with none of the blurring it so cried out for. As we waited for our dandelion surprise or whatever, he announced, "I've never had a drop of alcohol or any drug or a cigarette in my life."

"But you're forty," I said, "How is that possible? What happened in the '80s? Coke? Wine coolers? Anything?"

"It is possible because I am incredibly stubborn," Rafe said with a self-satisfied smile.

Then he launched straight into a story. "When I

was younger, I always had relationships with much older women. When I was seventeen, my lover was a forty-nine-year-old woman, Japanese, elegant, beautiful. One day we were in bed and she said, 'Stick your thumb up my ass, please, stick your thumb up my ass.'"

"And I said, 'I can't stick my thumb up the ass of an angel.' Now, of course I know that's exactly what you need to do." He leaned back with that smile again.

I pushed my dandelions around my plate.

"Now tell me what you like in bed," he said.

I mumbled, "Eh, no thanks, don't feel like going into—"

"Don't be shy," he commanded. "Tell me what you want. I like when women tell me."

My mind raced, and not toward sex with him. Do vegans eat dessert? Could we get the check after the dandelions? I was torn between throwing money down to signal that it was *not* a date, and the desire to make him pay for torturing me. How could he not get that I wasn't interested, that I was, in fact, repulsed?

After dinner, he insisted on walking me to the subway, where he pulled me toward him and pawed my hips. Seeing me cringe, he asked, "Does this make you uncomfortable?" with that horrible smile.

"Yes! Very! I don't know you!"

I pulled away, but he wouldn't let go and leaned in to kiss me. He was holding my arms tight.

I looked him in the eye and said, "I am not going to sleep with you. Let go of me."

He said, "Don't worry, I'm being a good boy. I'm not asking for that."

I said, "Good. Now let me go."

As I ran down the subway steps, he asked me to call him to say I got home safely. I did not comply.

He texted me an hour later, "R U alive?"

I answered, "Yes. Sorry for not calling. Goodnight."

He immediately texted back, "So should I be ragingly turned on by you?" That was followed by four more "sexy" texts.

I turned off my phone and went to sleep.

Two days later, he I.M.ed me on Facebook to let me know that he had been fantasizing about me. I didn't respond.

He continued to I.M. me, prompting the following exchange:

6:20 P.M. RAFE

oh well...i get a vibe of fading away
so be it

6:39 P.M. SANDY

yeah, sorry. you kinda creeped me out. you seem like a nice guy, but the sex talk is really not working for me.

6:39 P.M. RAFE

hahaha

creeped you out, bored me out
you seem nice but frazzled and the wistful
surrender of your allure was not working for me

6:40 P.M. SANDY

you be well

6:41 P.M. RAFE

i need a girlfriend, and then a wife, who believes in
her own power of seduction

That night, I blocked him from my Facebook page.
He sent a text:

"Oh. The cruelest cut of all! You de-friended me
on Facebook! NOW I will need therapy. I was getting
through it until this point."

I didn't respond. Three days later, he sends:

"Sorry to have reacted harshly but calling someone
creepy doesn't usually bring out the best in them."

I looked at his message in dismay. How had it
become my job to bring out the best in him? And
how would this ever end? I hated to let him win, but
I changed I.M. services and my cell phone number.
Only recently did I finally forgive my friend for
introducing me to this drummer whose different
beat was, in fact, stalking.

Sojourn in Hell Country

A sleepover without much sleep

Brian L., 28

I **"MET" THIS GIRL ON MATCH.COM,** despite a few red flags on her profile. She listed *regularly* as her drinking habits and added that she was a "weekend drunk."

But her pic was very cute and boredom overtook logic. And it's not like I don't party. We decided to go out in downtown Raleigh, and I drove out to Knightdale, a suburb, to pick her up.

She answered the door and looked *nothing* like her picture. For one, she was dressed like a fourteen-year-old. Her hair was actually in pigtails. She had black fingernails, a pentagram tattoo on her arm, and about 5,000 rings on her fingers.

She invited me in. On her mantel were a black candle, a skull, and the kinds of urns that hold ashes.

I should have run out the door and fled back to my apartment and my PlayStation. But I was curious, so I stuck around.

She put a six-pack of Natural Light into her Hello Kitty book bag, and we left. In the car, she said I was the first person she'd met off of Match whom she didn't already know. She also mentioned that she'd signed up for eHarmony and filled out the personality profile and that they'd *given her her money back.* Apparently, they had no confidence that they would *ever* find a match for her, so they went ahead and gave her a refund. Talk about a blow to the old ego. Online dating, the haven of crazies, can't even find a match for you?

In the car, she asked whether I'd mind if she cracked open a Natty Light, because she needs to put a few down before she goes out due to her agoraphobia. I mumbled something about North Carolina's open container law, but she was already sucking one down.

First stop was the apartment of a friend of hers. The friend was cuter *and* less crazy *and* we interacted better. But that was not my fate. We got stoned with the friend, then my date and I went to a bar called the Red Room, a decent place, but very crowded. And the lighting was, well, red. So there was this loud music playing, with people dancing bathed in red light. This particular evening, there was a gaggle of sailors in full attire. The atmosphere gave this feeling of Halloween. My possibly devil-worshipping date was writhing on me in a fascinating way. I thought to myself, I'm dancing in hell tonight—and I like it!

On the dance floor, she asked if she could come home with me. Once I agreed, she got weirder, as if I had let her "in" somehow.

HER: Do you have toothpaste?

ME: Um . . . who doesn't have toothpaste?

HER: Should we pick up pancake stuff?

ME: Um . . . are you going to want pancakes in the morning?

HER: No, I don't eat in the morning.

ME: Then let's not.

HER: Ooh! Do you want lasagna? I made some tonight. We could go pick it up at my house!

ME: Um . . . *No?*

We left the Red Room and she wanted to go to another bar, Hi 5. There she tells me she once made seven thousand dollars by letting a dude punch her in the face. And that she then cashed in an additional twelve thousand by selling the videotape as a porno.

I ran into a female friend at Hi 5 and she gave me a big, drunken hug. I felt a twinge of flame at the back of my neck—I could tell that Satan was pissed off. She grabbed my hand and led me out of the club.

We went back to my apartment. She rushed into the bathroom and was overjoyed to find that I did indeed have toothpaste. She came in and sat on my bed, crossing her legs like we were playing truth-or-dare at a slumber party.

She asked me a few questions about my past. To one of my answers, she responded, "At least you've never gotten pissed off and killed someone."

ME: Haha. And you have?

HER: Yeah, why do you think I left Long Island?

ME: No, seriously, you killed someone?

HER: Yeah, but I served my time.

ME: Who was it?

HER: An ex-boyfriend.

ME: Uh, how long did you serve?

HER: Three years of a fifteen-year sentence.

ME: So it was a manslaughter charge?

HER: Yeah.

ME: You're not going to kill me, are you?

HER: Not unless you piss me off!

I did *not* sleep well that night. The next morning, she noted that I left my checkbook out and told me I shouldn't do that—I mean, who knows what psycho would see it out and take it. I thanked her for the advice.

BLIND DATE OFFENSE #12
Unashamedly confessing to a life of crime

Freshman Year

Landing the dream guy

Gwen N., 19

MY FIRST BLIND DATE WAS, to tell the complete truth, my first date period. And I was eighteen years old. Could it get more pathetic, you ask? Why yes! The setter-upper was my mother!

It happened at that cultural moment when parents got onto Facebook. It was as if moms and uncles materialized in our dorms and dining halls and joined our conversations. I didn't think it could happen to me until a guy I had a huge crush on in high school texted me: "ur mom tried to friend me, ok if i ignore?"

I thought no way, my mom can barely e-mail. But somehow she'd gotten on there, and she was asking all my friends if they liked the White Stripes. Fortunately, she moved on from cyberstalking the youth to reuniting with long-lost friends. She found her college roommate Tracey, and the two of them got the idea to set me up with Tracey's son, Liam. My mom told me about him, then used the "Suggest a friend" feature to push us together.

Liam seemed a little nerdy. His pic was clearly from his high school yearbook, and his most recent FB activities were becoming a fan of Abraham Lincoln and posting a link to a video of whales. But he was kind of cute. I told my mom I'd meet him and Facebook-messaged him my digits. He called up on a Saturday morning and invited me to a baseball game two weeks hence. I said yes and we hung up.

I told my roommate Amber about the date, adding, "I know, how lame is that to get set up by my mom?" She looked at Liam's FB profile and said it was nice of me to make my mom happy and what time did I want to go to the bars.

• • •

I was still getting used to the dating rituals—mating rituals really—of college. I hadn't had boyfriends in high school, just hookups and friendships with guys. (My guy friends dated girls prettier than me who they couldn't talk to and complained about.) Having the sex and the conversation with the same person never happened for me in high school, and I'd hoped it would be different in college.

So far it was worse. I'd hooked up a few times with guys who then avoided eye contact in the dining hall. I had no guy friends at all. I had female friends, but none I'd chosen. They were friendships of geography—everyone on my dorm's hall.

We were mostly freshwomen, and we traveled in a pack. Thursday, Friday, and Saturday nights, we'd get ready together. We blasted music, borrowed clothes and makeup, talked about which guys were hot, maybe passed around a bottle, a cigarette, a joint. A few of us sneaked in a little discussion of a book or a class while we primped. These preliminaries were almost always the most fun part of the evening for me.

Then we'd go to one of three dive bars near school and try to hook up with someone. More often, I was cheering on a friend in her hook-up, but occasionally I too would "get lucky."

The Saturday on which I'd made the date with Liam was the worst sort of night. I was talking to this guy who was a senior and in a band. The other girls were cheering me on for a change, telling me he was a good score. So I drank two more beers than I wanted, acted interested in his microscopic descriptions of *Halo IV,* missed the last shuttle bus back to the dorm—and then watched him leave with this blonde sorority bimbo at 3:30!

My friends were long gone, and I trudged the mile home alone, bloated and depressed. It was so grim that I quit partying for almost two weeks—turned over a total minileaf. I spent a lot of time in the library, wrote some lame poetry, reread Hermann Hesse.

Two weeks later, I was still in the funk and tired of it. I took a long walk around the lake Saturday, but it didn't work. I walked into my dorm room around 6:00 and Amber was smoking a joint with our neighbors Pauline and Jen. I asked for a hit. They all did a double-take because I don't usually smoke. I don't like how it separates me from myself, but right then I wanted distance.

We passed the blunt around. We somehow got on the subject of parents. Mine were the only ones who'd stayed married. Jen hadn't seen her dad since junior high, and she said her mother was totally bitter, she like hated men. We were silent for a while.

> I don't like how smoking separates me from myself, but right then I wanted distance.

"It's kind of hard to imagine being married, isn't it?" I ventured.

"Who'd want it? Women don't need marriage anymore," said Pauline.

We agreed how women get screwed when they let themselves get dependent, and then I asked them, "But do any of you think it's strange that instead of boyfriends, we have sex with guys from our classes and then act like it didn't happen?" I thought about confessing that my baseball game date the next day with Liam would be the first actual date I'd ever had, but I didn't.

"That's what being young is for!" Jen said. "Why should guys have all the fun?"

Pauline chimed in, "It's this myth that women get all attached and needy, that we can't enjoy sex for sex's sake. Fuck that! I *love* sex."

"Let's do shots!" Amber yelled. She swirled and suddenly there were tiny glasses and a pretty bottle of brown whiskey in her manicured fingers. I flashed on her as a good wife and hostess some day as she handed around the shots. "To sex!" she cried out merrily.

"To sex!" I answered with the others. My chest loosened with a hopeful whoosh as the liquor warmed it. I didn't feel so separate this time. I merged with the girlfriends. We got dressed in leisurely increments—ten minutes of talking, two minutes of pulling clothes off hangers, four minutes of leaning over the dresser into the mirror applying eyeliner as a group, back down on the bed for another round of shots, a group shout-along to Rihanna "ella ella eh eh eh," then some shoe-borrowing.

For once, I was the one riding herd to the bars, yanking the others off my bed by their jean-jacketed arms. Walking into the Vouz, our first bar of the night, I felt a part of the roving sex team more than I ever had before. I finally understood how sex was a logical extension to sensual pleasures, like moving your body to music and laughing and gazing at attractive people in the bars' dark light. Sex was floating through the Vouz like smoke we could all breathe in.

I felt that I'd grasped something about the universe, and the universe confirmed it. For the first time in my life, guys hit on me. They looked, they smiled, a few walked over, one bought me a beer. It was truly unprecedented.

The one who bought me the beer seemed brain-damaged and Amber rescued me with a text. "Oh shit, excuse me," I said, making a worried face as I read, "Run away now."

I strode off and rejoined the girls at the bar. "Check it out, all these smokin' guys are like, 'Hey Gwen!'" Jen said, laughing with a slightly scary edge and shoving my upper arm. I didn't want her to attack me, so I murmured, "No, they're not," pushing her arm weakly.

"They so totally are," said Pauline, then to Jen: "Maybe she's ovulating. Men don't even know why they respond to ovulators."

"Not that you don't look cute, Gwen," she added. She and Jen went to the bathroom.

Amber put her arm around my shoulder and said, "You have the power. You pick them. Remember that." She was the sweetest one on the hall. I was lucky she was my roommate.

At that very moment, the most ridiculously hot guy in the whole college walked in. "Jason Dole," Amber and I both fake-drooled like Homer Simpson at the same time and then collapsed laughing into each other.

He was in my drawing class. I'd never actually conversed with him.

In class I'd stare at him as he drew the models. Tall, thick dark hair, blue eyes, big shoulders. I may have thought of him that way, like a collection of parts, because I studied him in that anatomical context.

LESSON #17

"Give him some milk for free, but suggest that other kinds might be bought."

I wanted to understand the power of that beauty. What are the regular-looking people all worshipping on the screens and the billboards, and occasionally, in real life? Is it really just symmetry?

I'm not going to say Jason's entrance into the Vouz was like a movie where everybody falls silent, but I was not the only one who noticed him come in. Jason looked around slowly.

He walked toward us, and my butt cheeks tightened. I whispered, "Amber alert; Amber alert" in her ear, because she's a million times hotter than me. I could tell by the way she arranged her body against the bar that she thought he was headed for her, too.

But he totally ignored her and spoke right to *me*. For the first time ever. There'd never been one "hey" or "can I borrow your pen" outside of class, none of those simple ways a person acknowledges you if he has registered your existence.

Not that I could mind that now: Up close, his beauty glowed even brighter. I was unnerved by the lack of anything imperfect to connect with. Amber's pep talk now seemed sweet, but absurd. He held the reins, all the cards, my evening in his elegant hands.

I stared up at him and waited.

"How's it going?"

"Fine, Jason, how're you?"

"Good. Great, Wen-dy?" he said tentatively.

"Gwen. Close!" I giggled as if he'd cracked a stellar joke. Amber sidestepped away, then gave me an amazed smile and a thumbs-up behind his back. I nodded back. She knew I wasn't going to introduce her; and I'd have totally slunk away if it was her he'd smiled upon. That's how it worked.

"Aw, I knew that, Gwen," he said, swinging his amazing body closer to mine to punch my arm. Then he couldn't think of anything to say. We smiled at each other like morons. A less hot, nerdier guy would have offered to buy me a two-dollar beer.

I finally made a stupid remark about drawing class. His vague response made me wonder if he even knew I was in that class. We laughed about what a dork the teacher was and got a little conversation groove going. I laughed too hard and watched his mouth move, had another beer. He touched my knee with his. It felt like my turn to decide where we'd touch next. I rolled some of my thigh into his.

"How about I walk you home?" he said.

I excused myself to ask Amber if she could sleep somewhere else, and she high-fived me and said of course, and whispered that there were condoms in her top drawer.

I wasn't really there on the walk. I was already in the next day telling the story to Amber, Pauline, and Jen. Jason was literally our shorthand for "hot guy," like "he's no Jason" or "he approaches Jasonness." Imagining their screams, I smiled up at him, memorizing his face from close range. He pulled his arm around my shoulder.

That little demi-hug was the peak of the night. Four seconds after we got in my room, Jason pulled his shirt and jeans off and rolled onto his back on my bed. I wasn't sure what to do; it was like he was displaying his heavenly body for me to admire. So I looked down, smiling stupidly, expecting him to reach for me or say something. But he just smiled up at me in his underpants and socks.

I laid down next to him in my clothes and scooched closer. He rolled his head toward mine. We "kissed," I guess you'd call it: His tongue was like a walrus that had been shot with a tranquilizer dart, lurching up periodically, then lying still. He pulled my hand onto his crotch, then pushed my face down into . . . how to name it . . . into his rubbery pink mass that didn't smell great. I tried to render it functional with my hands and mouth. I sighed and rolled away when I heard him snore.

I stared at the ceiling for a while, then walked down the hall to pee and brush my teeth. I was the only one at the long line of stained sinks. The fluorescent lights were turned down to firefly green late at night.

I crawled under the sheet and lay on my side, studying the sleeping form of Jason. For the first time that night, I felt like I did in class. He was back to being an aesthetic object. My head muscles relaxed into the freedom from having to talk to him.

I cheered silently, as if to the girls. "Jason Dole! In my bed!" It didn't work. I was so tired. Something tapped at my mind as I went under, something about the next day.

● ● ●

My cell phone woke me. The sun was hot in the stuffy room, and I was sweaty. "Hmmm?" I grunted into the phone. Jason sighed impatiently.

"Good morning, Gwen! It's Liam. I should be there in thirty minutes. Just wanted to give you a little heads-up."

Right, the thing at the edge of my mind. Just the first date of my whole life. I rolled onto my other side, away from Jason. "Right! Liam! Hey, take your time, I guess I overslept a little."

"No problem. Should I shoot to get there in an hour instead? We should still make the first pitch."

"Thanks, Liam. That would be better. Bye."

"Great. Should I pick you up any coffee or anything?"

"Thank you, that would be awesome." I gave him the address.

"Okay. See you soon."

I put down my phone and put my hand on Jason's muscled back. I was ready for a thrill, but didn't feel it, which was just as well. I shoved him. He didn't move.

I shook his shoulder lightly. "Look, I'm sorry, Jason, but you have to get out of here. I totally forgot someone's coming here to pick me up. He'll be here in half an hour."

"What time is it?"

"9:43."

"Sorry, but I need to sleep more, uh, —."

He didn't remember my name. Nice.

"What do you mean?"

I cheered silently, as if to the girls. "Jason Dole! In my bed!" It didn't work. I was so tired.

He rolled onto his back and raised himself up on his elbows. His arms and shoulders bulged gorgeously. He turned his head from side to side. "Look, you have this thick comforter. Throw it over me, and I'll lie really flat." He flopped back onto the mattress.

He was actually not going to leave. I buried my rage to gnaw on later. Now I had to deal.

I grabbed corners of the comforter and flung it up, watching the puff settle down over probably the most beautiful person who would ever be in my bed.

"What does it look like?" he asked from underneath.

"The Shroud of Turin. You have to turn your head sideways."

He did and it worked. It looked like a slightly rumpled, unoccupied bed. "Good. Okay, you don't have to turn your head yet," I said, but he had already fallen back to sleep.

I rushed back down the hall and into a long shower. My tired brain slogged over my life. Does Liam spend every Friday and Saturday night pursuing sex with someone new? I crouched down to soap my toes and tried to imagine what it would be like if love and sex came together. It made me think about my parents, so I got out of the shower fast.

What did I want Liam to be like? I pulled on a sundress and looked at the slope of Jason. I used my fingers to tick off "Remembers my name. Can have a conversation. Can kiss. Decent in bed." The only desirable similarity with Jason would be looks.

Jason rolled onto his side and farted demystifyingly. I opened the window, heard a knock at the door. Liam? Who doesn't call when they're approaching? Oh god, it was really smelly.

"Jason, roll onto your back and turn your head," I hissed, snapping the comforter up and down over him. "Just a sec, I'll be right there. I'm all ready to go!"

I looked back at the room. The bed was convincingly flat. I'd have to text Amber to warn her that Jason was still in our room.

I grabbed my purse, cracked the door, and pushed myself out like toothpaste. Liam was right there, ready to be invited in.

"Hey, don't want to be late," I said, subtly herding him away from the door with my body.

He smiled and thrust a coffee at me. He was tall. His pants were too small, but not in the cool indie rock way.

"So nice to m-meet you, G-g-g-gwen." He hadn't stammered on the phone.

"It's chilly. You should bring a jacket." I protested that I never got cold, and he argued with me. "We're right at your room. G-g-g-rab one; you'll be g-g-g-glad later." G's were especially bad. Here's a guy who remembers my name, but can't say it.

"Okay, okay, I'll get a jacket." I punched in the lock combination and slid back into the room. He squeezed in behind me and looked right at my bed. Jason didn't have his head all the way turned, but I suppose it could have looked like a pillow under the comforter. I turned on the radio, in case any more sounds wafted from Mr. Body Function. "Maybe hear some pregame wrap-up," I babbled. I grabbed my jacket, pushed Liam out ahead of me, and turned up the radio to disturb Jason's sleep.

I had a nice day with Liam. I grew used to the stuttering, and to him keeping score on a sheet like a twelve-year-old. It was the most I'd ever enjoyed watching a sport, the first time I was happy that "our" team won. Liam opened the car door for me and bought my hot dog and beer. He knew a lot about stuff I'm interested in. He was nice.

It was easy to talk to him. He was more like me than Jason, certainly, and more like me than the girls on my hall. He'd be a good boyfriend. We said we'd stay in touch.

The day was fun enough that I forgot to text Amber. So she came back to our room just as Jason was waking up, around noon. He'd invited her into my bed, she told me, looking at me sadly.

"What did you say?"

Amber shrieked. "What do you think?! God! Of course I said no. What am I, like brunch?"

I told her I wouldn't have minded, and I'm pretty sure that's true.

BLIND DATE OFFENSE #123
Overstaying your welcome

Stinky Pete

When past and present collide

Peter Z., then 44

I ONLY WENT BECAUSE MY FRIEND SARA kept pushing. My second divorce had just come through, and the prospect of any two people sticking it out for a lifetime seemed almost absurd. Some days I thought the whole wedded world was deluded; other days I thought the problem was me. I simply couldn't muster the right combination of self-blinding and tongue-biting and generosity that marriage took. So went my defeated assessment.

But Sara kept talking Felicia up. She worked as an art therapist with senior citizens. Since I struggled constantly not to snap at my own aging parents, I couldn't imagine how someone spent all day with strangers who were that enfeebled, stubborn, and frightened. Surely someone so patient could put up with me.

Sara assured me that Felicia was no sanctimonious saint, though. She was funny; she loved to dance; she could curse in five languages; she crushed all comers at Scrabble. Sara sold me partway, and that brainless duo of lust and hope did the rest. What can I say, I don't like being alone.

We made a date at a tiny new restaurant in a not-yet-gentrified neighborhood: a middle-aged urbanite's adventure. The evening of the date, I felt guilty for sending a woman to this neighborhood alone, and left a little early so I could intercept her and help her find the place. As I drew near, I saw a small, slim woman with long, curly hair and a determined walk coming my way. I thought, Mmmm, I hope that's her.

It was. She was beautiful, gracious, with big kind eyes. As we made that first awkward chat, she brought a sense of calm into our nervousness. She assured me she'd heard about this restaurant and had also wanted to try it, and that she loved this neighborhood.

We smiled at each other for too long, caught ourselves, laughed and went in. The hostess sat us at a small table next to a long table full of guys. We settled in and said nice things about Sara and then drifted to the other people in our lives we cared about. Felicia praised everyone she talked about.

The waiter had been over three times to take our order and each time we apologized, but returned to our conversation without looking at the menu.

Then, suddenly: *"Stinky Pete! No fuckin' way!"* The guttural shout rang through the small room. It seemed so distinct from what was happening between Felicia and me that I didn't even register my own rugby nickname. I stayed focused on Felicia.

"Check it out, Shithead! Now he won't talk to the likes of us." Much laughter. Felicia glanced over at the table full of men. "Um, they're all looking at you—Stinky Pete?" She giggled.

"But that can't be," I said. I'd played rugby twenty-five years ago, 300 miles away. I turned.

It was. They were balder, fatter, and redder of face, but I was looking at Shithead, Headboard, Frank the Hooker, Danny Donuts, Stupid Pete, Gamblin' Dave, and Psycho, about half the starting lineup of my college team sitting around a platoon of empty beer pitchers.

My hand tightened around my water glass. I glanced at Felicia, then back at the former boys. Finally, I responded. "Holy crap, it's you guys. What are you doing here?" I realized that sounded unfriendly. Felicia was studying me. "How are you all? Great to see you!"

"I *told* you that was him, same ugly mug!" shouted Psycho, never one of my favorite teammates.

"Come join us, have a beer!" said Headboard (né Edward).

"I, we, uh . . ." I looked helplessly at Felicia. I craved a drink ferociously. I took a deep breath and stood up.

"Hey guys, this is Felicia. Felicia, this is, uh,

Edward and uh . . ." I didn't remember Shithead's real name. ". . . And the other guys from my old rugby team. Wow! And I would love to catch up, guys, but this is sort of a special night for us, and so I can't right now. How long are you all in New York? What are you *doing* here?" This was the conversation I didn't want to be drawn into, but it was too strange that my rugby team from the University of Pittsburgh was in a restaurant in Red Hook, Brooklyn.

Danny Donuts, of all people, rescued me. He'd picked up a few social graces since the days he used to steal everyone's food and beer. "Me and Headboard live in Brooklyn now, the others came to visit. Here's my card—give me a call tomorrow. Most everyone will still be around. Great to see you, bro. Enjoy your date."

"I *told* you that was him, same ugly mug!" shouted Psycho, never one of my favorite teammates.

Psycho and a few of the others grumbled that I'd gotten off the hook too easily, but they finally turned away from us.

"That was sweet, but it's fine if you want to join them," Felicia said.

"No! I mean, thanks, but I don't want to. I don't want to go back there. I like it here better."

I studied her face. Had Sara told her I was sober three years, or what a drunk I'd been before? Felicia hadn't ordered a drink either; was that coincidence or sensitivity? The guys' banter, suddenly in focus, was like the sound track to my wasted life, my fake relationships, and self-deception.

"Hey," Felicia said softly. "I'm not really hungry. Let's take a walk instead."

My heart lurched out of its cave. "Really? But we're in the middle of nowhere."

"We're somewhere," she said, and stood up and apologized to the waiter. I quickly waved good-bye to the team, and Felicia and I walked the deserted streets for three hours, sharing more than I ever had on a first date. It wasn't until I was walking her to her door that she asked, "So why were you called Stinky Pete?"

The answer was disgusting, but I didn't even consider lying. She laughed. I asked if I could see her the next night and she said "Duh."

We've been married ten years. Everything I thought I saw in her that first night is really there.

It's Medical

Years ago, a first date told me, "I have anger issues." I'm a sympathetic sort, and I was very young. "Poor guy," I thought, "how brave of him to admit he has a problem." The next few dates included tirades at blameless waiters, tirades against drivers who slowed down at yellow lights, tirades about the shoddy construction wherever we went. (He was a foreman on upscale houses.) The rants were usually funny, which briefly distracted me from their nastiness.

But on our fourth date, I told him gently that his bile was making my head hurt. Could he tone it down any? He played the medical card again, told me how hard he was working on those anger issues. Then he asked if I thought we should do couples counseling.

I declined and pondered, not for the last time, the line between "psychological issue sufferer" and "jerk."

Maniac

The universe doesn't always say "yes" back

Megan M., 36

I MET SETH WHEN I WAS NINETEEN, and I was thirty-three when we divorced. The most lethal stressor on our marriage was, in my opinion, his depression, which crushed his libido flat. Just as I entered my purported sexual peak, I got rejected by my husband. He was only the second man—boy, really, at the time—I'd ever slept with.

By the time Seth finally moved out, I hadn't had sex in more than two years. Dismayingly, he had, while we were still married, with an acquaintance of mine. I later heard thirdhand that she'd found him a tepid lover and moved on in search of hotter adultery. That cheered me up.

Once he and the cat were finally gone (I kept the dog), it took me another six months to think about dating. My life was so radically changed, and my

therapist was encouraging me to pay attention and
process. Introspection made more sense to me than
acting out, the post-divorce course most of my friends
had taken. My friend Dana called it "the post-divorce
boogie," always swinging her hips front-to-back when
she said the phrase. She and some others thought I
should be lunging at sexual experience, but I didn't
have that confidence or knowledge.

I'd never lived alone before. After the fights and
sulks and despair, it mostly seemed wonderfully
quiet and free. I work at home as a ghostwriter and
journalist; now I could do anything whenever I wanted.
I didn't have to cheer him up or take care of the stupid
relationship. I felt like a nurse relieved of her most
draining patient.

But other times—Sunday afternoons especially—it
felt like I didn't exist without someone to talk to. Did
the dog's ears count? I scratched them and asked her,
"Sadie, you hear the tree falling in the forest, dontcha,
girl? I'm here, right? Who needs her person? Who?
You do!" It wasn't just our dog-human relationship I
discussed with Sadie, but also my fears about money,
my rage at Seth for the wasted years, what being
thirty-three and single meant.

Dana looked aghast when I told her about my
conversations with the dog. "Babe, you gotta get out
of that house. Dress up, have some fun, get laid." My
therapist agreed, not explicitly with the get laid part,

but she did say that I should try saying yes to more things. It would help me shed Seth's negativity and to figure out what I like. I realized how much I'd avoided because Seth, a depressive, might not like it.

• • •

I threw out my yes to the world, but sadly, the world did not seem to hear. Dana noticed my yes echoing back at me forlornly and did some legwork. She then asked if I was ready to meet her friend Allan—a writer, smart, never married, a couple years older than me, a lot of fun. He lived 150 miles away but came into town a lot.

MOTHER KNOWS BEST

LESSON #63

"The best way to get over someone is to get under someone else."

"Yes," I said. I Googled him and he turned out to be a biggish-deal writer. I Google-imaged him and he looked attractive. I fantasized in a weirdly vague way, like an adolescent virgin. I'd never dated; I didn't have an ideal date in mind, nor the conversation, the activity, the romance, kiss, or sex.

Dana reminded me that he'd know what to do. She also picked my outfit. (It flashed through my mind that maybe the person I'd like to marry—the one who'd taken the best care of me—was Dana.)

We met at his hotel's bar. I was there first, eating peanuts and watching CNN when he walked in, rubbing the back of his neck. He was very tall and thin, bent slightly inward. He had on a gray suit. He looked elegant, harried, worldly. I felt like a rube, out of my league.

He smiled when he saw me, and suddenly I felt myself turning from rube to pretty ingenue. I smiled back and he rushed over, pouring words at me.

"You must be Megan good to meet you sorry I'm late, oh this place is awful TVs are taking over the world let's go down the street." He paid the bartender for my drink and ushered me out of the hotel with his hand on the small of my back. It was like a glamorous movie, sweeping out golden doors and down the sidewalk. After a few blocks, we went down steps into a dark, red bar; he scooted us into a semicircular booth flanked by beautiful wooden screens and ordered a bottle of wine.

I asked about his latest book and what he was working on now, and he was eloquent and entertaining. I liked looking at him and listening to the sound of his voice. He drew me out, mostly on the topic of my divorce. About thirty minutes after we got there, though, he cupped his hand over his eye, tilting his head back. He kept on talking, but he'd stopped looking at me. His uncupped eye was almost closed, upturned to the ceiling.

"Are you okay?"

"Yes. Well, no. But it's all right. I have chronic pain. Nothing works, I've tried a million treatments.

Right now, I have sort of a migraine, but it's not going anywhere. So I'd like to stay here with you, if that's all right. I like you. I'm sorry about how I'm sitting. I know it must look strange but it helps a little." He rubbed my shoulder for a second with his free hand.

It's no accident I fell in love with a man who has major depression. I hope I've evolved some, but I think I'll always feel tender toward the hurt ones. Allan's chronic pain was annoying on one level, as I'd been enjoying the glamorous stranger-and-ingenue vibe. But it also drew me closer. I didn't know how to seduce, but I did know how to comfort.

Plus it was fascinating to the journalist in me. No orthopedist or neurologist or chiropractor or acupuncturist or massage therapist or hypnotist could cure the pain that Allan felt during half of his waking hours.

"You long for another sensation to distract you," he explained, rolling his head forward to look at me while he kneaded his temple. "I don't think I'd have become a sex addict without the chronic pain," he added.

The journalist blinked. "A sex addict?" Dana hadn't mentioned this.

"Yeah, I'm in a twelve-step program for it."

My god, I thought, the distribution was so unfair! Some people go without any sex for years, while others are snorting it up like cocaine. "What's the goal of the program?" I asked.

"Not celibacy," he laughed and touched my arm. "To be rid of the compulsion and to stop doing reckless, self-destructive things." He'd pushed closer to me on the round leather seat.

What things? I thought, and simultaneously, I don't want to know.

There was silence. He looked at me, waiting.

"Um, so when did you get, uh, diagnosed as a sex maniac?"

"Sex *addict*," he laughed. "It's not something anyone diagnoses." He touched my hair, and I found my head pushing into his hand like a cat's. His compulsion was the opposite of my ambivalence or fear or whatever was keeping me from the post-divorce boogie.

"A sex addict?" Dana hadn't mentioned this.

I had no idea what to say or do. I stared at him.

"Do you want to go to my hotel room?" he asked.

Wow, that was easy. "I don't know."

"Hmm. Well, why wouldn't you?" he asked.

"Um, I don't know anything about you except you're a sex maniac—"

"Addict," he said, a little irritably this time. "You also know what I've written, that we hit it off—and that you need to say yes more," he added teasingly. I'd told him about my divorce and my new life plan.

"Okay. Yes. But I may not want to do anything and I may want to leave, all right?"

"Of course. Just because I'm a sex maniac doesn't mean I'm going to tie you up. Unless you want me to."

"No thank you."

"All righty then."

Back in the hotel room, he was very sweet and gentle. We made out for a while on the edge of the bed, on top of the covers. He took off some of my clothes, but I kept on my bra and panties. "It's fine," he murmured, "but why?"

I mumbled into his shoulder. "I've only slept with two guys my whole life: my high school boyfriend and my husband."

"Now *that's* kinky," he breathed, doing something with his right hand that felt very good.

Nevertheless, I decided to leave after another half-hour of kissing and stroking. "Thank you," I said at his door. "This was really fun." He agreed and said that we should do it again, then he kissed me good-bye tenderly. "Next time I'll be braver," I promised.

I felt lucky that he'd been my first post-divorce kiss, and looked forward to seeing him when he came back into town the following month. After he arrived—I knew he had plans with Dana plus another public event—I waited eagerly for his call.

It didn't come. I called and left him a message, and the next day I texted him. Nothing. Ever. Dana stayed mad at him for months.

I managed to mostly stay mad, too, but I can't deny a crisis of confidence. This had been my remount, nay, my first mount onto the dating horse. I'd said yes to a self-absorbed, pain-riddled sex maniac. And, so, what—he was too good for me? Didn't he get that I was being generous as well as adorably adventurous, how big a deal it was that we'd made out in his hotel room? I hated the quick rise and slow fall of hope, the rejection, the lack of closure, the not knowing. Three years later, I'm still trying those yesses, and the dating saddle is still awfully uncomfortable.

BLIND DATE OFFENSE #27
Quoting Dr. Phil

My Blind Date Went Blind!

The case was never solved

Audrey T., then 22

IT WAS THE LATE '60S, and I was in graduate school at Columbia. Somebody on my floor in International House fixed me up—one of those things where he asked if I would go to dinner with his out-of-town friend as a favor. The friend wanted a date to take to a nice restaurant on Saturday night.

I was fresh out of an all-girls college and pretty much game for anything, so I said yes.

Saturday night rolled around, and Warren came to pick me up. He had a round, freckled face with sandy reddish hair. Not terribly tall and definitely not my type. I wasn't repulsed, but nor was I thrilled.

We took a cab to the restaurant, a well-known Italian place in Times Square. It was packed.

We had pasta and unmemorable conversation. I do remember—and this is relevant—that though we had wine with dinner, neither of us were drunk or stoned or anything.

And then suddenly, just after dessert arrived, he went pale. His freckles were standing out and sweat beaded on his forehead. His eyes squinted and he swung his head back and forth. He said, looking terrified, "I can't see."

"What do you mean you can't see?!"

He kept repeating "I can't see." He wiped his face with his napkin. Then he stood up and turned slowly. He'd already been to the bathroom and remembered vaguely where it was.

He wove among lots of tables, groping the backs of chairs and other diners as he shuffled across the room. He asked three waiters where the bathroom was and finally stumbled through the door, knocking over an empty chair just before he got there. The restaurant seemed to have fallen silent.

I sat there stunned, looking around as if someone out there might know what was going on. They looked at me like *I* was supposed to know. About ten minutes later, Warren emerged and slowly made his way back to the table, still squinting (and oblivious to the puzzled faces all around) but not as incapacitated.

As he sat down I said, "We'd better leave," and signaled the waiter.

The check came. Warren fumbled with his wallet, clearly couldn't see the denomination of the bills, so I went ahead and paid. I don't remember the amount, but I was a student, and this was one of those real New York restaurants—the kind of place you'd go to when your parents came to town. Annoyance overwhelmed my sense of empathy for a moment, I'll admit.

I took Warren out on my arm, hailing a cab and giving the address of his hotel. (I'd become the man on this date.) The ride was quite silent—there are only so many times you can ask if a person is okay! I walked him to his hotel and handed him off to a bellhop. I asked for his hotel number to check up on him, but when I called the next day he had already checked out.

Someone told me soon thereafter about a condition called hysterical blindness. I suppose that's what it was. I asked the friend who set us up about Warren, and he hadn't heard a word about it. Warren could see fine as far as he knew.

Shut Your Mouth!

When medical and dental emergencies collide
Tim K., 27

MY COLLEGE FRIEND RON set me up with a former roommate of his. He told me she was brilliant and sexy and had a car. We met at a darkened bar after I'd already had a few.

We talked over candles and strong drink. She was pretty enough and we had common interests, and we jabbered on happily. I was wasted and hungry, so I suggested we drive to her place and make dinner.

We stumbled into her kitchen and she flipped on a fluorescent light. I woozily grinned at her and when she smiled back, I saw that one of her front teeth was a very dark gray. It looked dead, rotted, like a zombie tooth still inexplicably among its living family. It looked like it would smell, and as soon as I thought that, I smelled it or thought I did.

I could look at nothing else. She clattered pots and

pans, and then I realized, suddenly sober, that I could not possibly eat across the table from her. I grabbed my cell phone, mumbled "vibrate," held up my pointer finger to excuse myself, and slipped into the next room. "Oh my god. Really? Of course." I felt a ping of worry for my imaginary friend. I was at that level of drunkenness where I believed my own lie.

Sincerely, I said, "I am so sorry, but I have to run." I bolted out the kitchen door. "I'll call you," I shouted over my shoulder.

> I was at that level of drunkenness where I believed my own lie.

The next day, she called to say that Ron was in the hospital after a serious car accident. She would drive us there. Ron, in the hospital? Without thinking, I said yes. The ride to the hospital wasn't too bad. The tooth corpse was on the driver's side. She seemed to believe my story from the night before and asked me if my friend who called, or vibrated, was okay.

We got into Ron's hospital room, and he was fine. He was getting out later that day. But Ron is a drama queen and he was milking the attention. As Zombie Tooth and I stood on opposite sides of his bed, Ron took each of us by the hand, looked soulfully back and forth, and said, "I am so glad that there was at least one good thing to come out of this."

She smiled at me and my eyes went to her mouth. I had no idea what my face was doing, but I did know it wasn't disfigured by something that any normal person would have dealt with at the dentist. I started to get mad. It was downright disrespectful to me to come out to meet me with rot in her mouth!

"Tim? Tim! What's wrong?" I heard Ron's voice. "Dude, you have this insane expression. What is it? What's going on?"

"It's just, I'm . . . I'm glad you're okay, Ron!" I said and ran out as if overcome with relief. And thank god for real that he was okay, so I didn't feel too guilty avoiding both of their phone calls for the next few weeks.

BLIND DATE OFFENSE #75
On part of setter-upper, failure to communicate make-or-break details

The Gift

Which eventually became a regift
Rosalie H., 32

WHAT CAN I SAY, I LIKE WEIRDOS. Always have. My girlfriends'll tell me about a guy who sang them a little song on their first date, or the one who fit a whole orange in his mouth. They wrinkle up their noses, expecting me to be appalled, and I'm like "Wait, you're saying you *don't* want to see this guy again?"

My friend Roy knows this about me, and so he set me up with this mad scientist pal of his, or that's how he billed him anyway. But the mad scientist talked about TV shows I don't watch and the renovations he's planning for his deck. Sometimes I wonder if normal people really are interested in the stuff they talk about or if they're all as bored as I am and just being polite.

In short, I got restless. So when the scientist asked me to come up to the lab and see what's on the slab, I said hells yeah.

We were poking around his basement and I saw a glass jar with something yellowish in it. I moved closer and saw a paw pad pressed against the glass, fur, and a stubby tail.

"It's a puppy, or would have been. The mother died and we extracted her pups, six of them, when I was in vet school," he said.

I picked up the jar and turned it, studying it from every angle. The head was at the bottom of the spiraled form. The side of the mouth was a black slit pressed flat against the jar's base.

"Would you like to have it?" he asked.

"A jar of dog? Of course I'd like to have it." That gift won him another date, but we fizzled soon after that.

I moved the jar all over my house, but never found the right place for it. In the kitchen was too macabre even for me. The bathroom was too crowded. In the bedroom it took too much surface area, and in the living room it made my niece cry. The next fellow I dated was a science teacher, and I gave it to him for his birthday.

The Sound of Seduction

PICK-UP LINE #89

"You must work in a library—you just increased my circulation."

"Dude, You're the Neurologist"

A very scrambled egg

Polly P., 31

I **WAS DOING MY MEDICAL RESIDENCY** in neurology, in
desolate Edmonton. It was miles away from where
I'd grown up in Montreal, where all my friends and
family were. All I did in Edmonton was work, sleep,
and shiver. Online dating was still very suspect back
in 2001, but I signed up anyway, starved for distraction
and body warmth.

I cast a wide net, since I was in the middle of
nowhere. A guy who seemed smart and funny wrote
from Toronto. He would be in town for a shareholders
meeting, would I like to meet? He had some sort of
financial job.

His name was Stu, and his picture was blurry. He
was fun on e-mail and we made plans pretty quickly.

I wanted to make the most of a rare night out, so we planned dinner and a movie. I picked the restaurant and he picked *Zoolander*. Not my first choice, but fine.

We recognized each other at the edge of the parking lot in the strip mall, smiled and shook hands. He was tall, bushy-haired, young looking. Within moments, however, I was thrown into confusion by his eyes. They tracked completely independent of each other, one steady, the other wandering. But never, as far as I could tell, did they look in the same direction. They weren't even the same color.

"It's a congenital ocular disorder. People tell me they get used to it."

I found that gracious and brave. My heart melted for him a bit. I wasn't attracted to him, but I resolved to enjoy his company. That wasn't hard. He had an odd mix of maturity and adolescence—an exuberant hippie who loved the stock market. He explained world markets to me better than anyone ever had, using the salt and pepper and silverware as visual aids. He also asked smart questions about neurology. And I did get used to the eyes, mostly.

Before I finished my wine, Stu called for the check, paid it, then excused himself for a "fresh-air break." He came back a few minutes later, and I drove us to the twenty-four–screen multiplex. We rode up and down five floors of elevators, past huge cardboard Will Ferrells on maroon-carpeted landings. We finally found

Zoolander. Stu dashed off for another fresh-air break, calling back, "You get the snacks! A big-ass tub of popcorn!"

He didn't get back till the previews were almost over. The theater had completely filled up, mostly with adolescents, while I stood there with a mail bin's worth of popcorn. I tried to keep my anger off my face as Stu strode up, smiling confidently. He tapped the pimply young usher and barked genially, "Get us two seats together! In the middle." The kid was terrified and fumbled for his flashlight, then darted his gaze back and forth between Stu's eyes.

"Sorry, excuse me, thank you, sorry, sorry," I muttered.

The usher shone his light down the rows of laps till he found two seats. We followed his beam across twenty comfortable people who had to stand up just as the movie started. "Sorry, excuse me, thank you, sorry, sorry," I muttered, as people crouched to accommodate our feet and butts. Stu was already shoveling in popcorn as we scooted across, dribbling it onto a number of unsuspecting heads.

Finally, we settled in and turned to the screen. It was very dark and quiet. Times and place names appeared in somber Courier typeface; ominous music stirred. "It's kind of cool that they'd start *Zoolander* this way," I whispered to Stu. A neighbor overheard and said, "This is *Training Day.*"

Stu groaned. "I don't want to see this," he announced loud enough to make a lot of people shush him. I stood up and pushed him back the way we came. "I don't either. Better to get out of here now," I hissed at him, pushing past the now-incredulous people who just sat down. Some laughed as they stood up for us again; most did not.

We got out into the lobby and Stu asked, either mock-irritated or actually irritated, "How could you have led us into the wrong movie? Who does that?"

I laughed. "Why is it my fault? I got us to the multiplex, you could have found *Zoolander*."

He widened his eyes and said indignantly, "Dude, *you're* the neurologist. And *I'm* baked!"

Aha! Now the fresh-air breaks made sense. As did the way he blithely bossed and bullied and acted like a lunatic, with utter entitlement. The way he didn't seem to focus. He was stoned! I had to laugh. I hadn't thought of any drugs besides NoDoz in a couple of years.

Instead of calling it a night, I said, "Let's rent another Ben Stiller movie. *Flirting with Disaster* is one of my favorites, and I'd like to see it again." He suggested we go to his hotel, but I felt safer in my apartment. There was an older couple next door who kept an eye on me.

We went into the living room and Stu plopped down. I slid in the disc. Stu, right behind me, said, "Where's the TV?"

I pointed to the fourteen-inch set I was standing right next to.

"That?" He squinted. "No way! I can't watch that!" He described his wall-mounted twenty-million-inch projector set, then hoisted himself up. He announced, "I'm taking the house tour" and walked into my coat closet.

It dawned on me that "I can't watch that" wasn't tech snobbery but a statement of fact. I'd been consistently slow to catch on to this guy's impairments—and dude, *I'm* the neurologist!

He backed out of the closet and headed down the hall. After a minute or so, I followed and found him lying on my bed. He patted the comforter next to him. "C'mon. It'll be fun." He smiled up at me sleepily, one eye almost shut.

I backed out into the hallway laughing. I planned how to tell him he had to go back to his hotel, then walked back into my bedroom. "Look, Stu—" I heard a snore. He looked even younger asleep. I sighed and went to make up my couch.

By the time I woke up the sun was high, and Stu was banging around in the kitchen. On the counter were a hunk of cheese, three apples, two tomatoes, a carton of eggs, and a tall spray can of oven cleaner.

"Stu. What are you doing?"

"I'm making us breakfast, dude! I'm starving!"

I pointed at the oven cleaner. "What's that for?"

He held the can close to his face and turned it, doubt in each eye. He kept the doubt out of his voice though: "Nonstick spray. For the world-famous Stu omelet. See?" The poison slid gleaming across my frying pan as he tilted it toward me.

"How about we go out to brunch?" I said calmly. "I know a place right near your hotel."

BLIND DATE OFFENSE #5
Poisoning your date

A CHEMICAL REACTION

Who doesn't want their blind date to start with a wordless "Yes"? A mutual "Oh you *are* cute" makes everyone on the date happy. But the key word is mutual. When the assent is not shared, chaos can ensue.

Not that attraction ever guarantees success. To paraphrase Billie Holiday, "cute" can make us do things that we know is wrong. It's certainly been known to spin dates in terribly wrong directions, especially when mixed with alcohol. Even Carl Jung called the erotic instinct "something questionable."

Once in a while, though, stupid libido does get things right, herding us past obstacles to a nicely fitting match.

The Odds Are Good, but the Goods Are Odd

"I can accept this situation"

Miriam T., 28

THE ODDS ARE GOOD, but the goods are odd. That's what they say about a girl's chances in Alaska, where there are supposedly ten men for every woman. I was living in a (surprise) cold apartment in a tiny village, compiling research about permafrost at a small data station. I worked with four much older married men from the closest university, eighty-five miles away. They went straight home from work. I didn't know anybody else.

I was surprised at how lonely I got in my apartment. I spent most evenings in the only bar in town, making small talk with hunters and fishermen who didn't seem to have bigger talk in them. I became a master of the monosyllabic conversation while watching hockey on the TV over the bar.

"Score?"

"One zip."

"We up?"

"For now."

"They'll choke."

"Henh."

It felt more intimate than it sounds, but it didn't banish my loneliness.

I'm going to call this a blind date story, even though Danny and I didn't get set up. The bar was very dark; it *felt* like a blind date. The cigarette smoke was so thick that the few lights that did work—the neon Coors sign, the forty-watt bulb over the pool table, the TV—were dimmed as if by fog.

On this one Tuesday night, I noticed a new fellow noticing me. He was tall and skinny, with a gauntness to his face. I liked his looks; I stared back. He lurked by the jukebox for ten minutes, then sat on the bar stool next to mine.

"What're you drinking?" His voice rasped pleasantly. He looked ageless in that Alaska way— rough voice, wild beard, leathery-red face from the wind—but he was probably around thirty.

"Beer," I said flirtatiously.

He ignored me, and called to the bartender, "Two bourbons." He turned back and smiled down at me, showing surprisingly white, straight teeth. "Beer won't warm you up." He handed me my glass, and threw about half of his down in one shot. "I'm Danny," he said, wiping the corners of his mouth with the back of his hand.

Danny's conversation sparkled no more than his townsmen's, but I liked the sound of his voice and how his body seemed aware, even intelligent. Like many men of few words, he seemed physically intuitive. I felt safe with him.

We talked unhurriedly about the permafrost and about his job as a salmon fisherman. I had already had two beers, and I am not a big person. He read my drunkenness perfectly. Toward the end of my bourbon, his knee "accidentally" brushed my thigh, and the touch raced up my leg, as hot as the bourbon felt going down. We kept the conversation limping along, but subtext roared up past text. Nobody had touched me in months.

He knew it, too. He saw that I wouldn't require much finessing. He laid money down on the bar and said, "Let's go." I bundled myself into my down coat and followed him to his pickup truck.

Ten minutes later, he was opening the unlocked door to a tiny, cold house. Two black Labs writhed and squirmed around our feet, their tongues thrusting up at us like jumping fish. He followed the dogs outside to the woodpile while I sat on the couch in my coat. I could see my breath. There wasn't much else to see in the room.

He brought in wood and fed the woodstove in his bedroom. Once the fire was going, he went to the tiny kitchen area, rinsed two glasses, and poured us each more bourbon. He allowed me one sip, then he grabbed my face and tongue-kissed me.

A vestigial ladylikeness surged up in me—what, no seduction?—but the bourbon beat it back down. We unzipped each other's coats and burrowed our hands into each other's sweaters, shirts, and long underwear. I gasped when he grazed my nipple and he pulled me up and into the bedroom, which had warmed up to maybe the low fifties.

The Sound of Seduction

PICK-UP LINE #13

"Nice pants, but they'd look better on the floor."

I barely saw the lay of the land before he turned off all the lights, just a brief glimpse of a half-barrel serving as a night table and a huge pile of blankets with black dog hair on them. In the dark, we peeled off our coats and boots and got under the covers to finish undressing. The blankets tented down from him kneeling between my legs and pulling my clothes off. He quickly worked his way down to my feet, which had been cold for the entire four months I lived in Alaska.

He tenderly pulled off both pairs of socks and rubbed my feet to warm them. I laid back, completely surrendered to this kindness. Then he lifted my foot up to his mouth and started licking the big toe. Nobody had ever done this to me. It tickled, not unpleasantly. His breath was very warm. He hadn't uncovered my deepest kink or anything, but it felt good.

Soon he was sucking the whole big toe, then the big toe plus its two neighbors. With three toes engulfed in the warm wet, I got turned on even though it kind of felt like stepping on a slug. The sensation teetered on the edge of sexy and some ridiculous opposite of sexy.

> He hadn't uncovered my deepest kink or anything, but it felt good.

Then Danny withdrew, leaving my damp foot cold in the night air. I looked down, but could only see the barest outline of him in the dark. He was on his knees, cradling my ankle and straight leg. I felt one of his arms move outside the blankets, and I heard a thump as something hit the bedside half-barrel. Drinking from a glass of water, I figured.

He pulled my foot back up to his mouth. He sucked on the same three toes, then opened wider. All five toes were in there, then the whole ball of my foot. His lips were stretched around the arch of my foot, and his tongue flickered all the way to my heel.

He felt me stiffen, and ran his hands up and down my thighs, wheezing a little to breathe around my foot. His hands helped me to relax, but my mind floated up to look down at this circus act. How did he do it? His mouth was so big, so soft and massaging. It was as if wet hands were rubbing my entire foot. It felt nice, but wrong somehow.

I pulled my hand up to my own mouth. I made a fist and pushed it past my lips, to figure out how one got a whole appendage in there. Meanwhile, he sucked and sucked, bobbing as if giving my foot a blow job. He began to moan.

My knuckles were caught in the portcullis of my teeth. So how in the world was Danny fellating my entire size-six foot?

I said "Oh my god" when I figured it out. Encouraged, he sucked faster. His mouth was soft, warm, huge—and toothless. I flashed on his perfect white teeth in the bar, his slightly sunken cheeks, and most sickening, the mysterious thump. In the dark, I imagined the dentures grinning at me from the bedside half-barrel, mocking my lust, my recklessness, and now my horror. I shuddered. He rubbed my calf.

I considered my situation. Danny and I were now intimate. We would have to talk once he took my foot out of his mouth, the mouth that would collapse into itself like an old apple. It'd be dark though, and he'd pop the teeth back in quickly, probably. Surely he'd do that before we kissed, right? The teeth would be cold from the room. Would that sting, cold dentures hitting hot gums? There was so much to contemplate.

His mouth pulsed gently around my arch. We were intimate; I could not escape that. I laid back on the pillow and smelled the wood burning, the dogs, the hint of fish. It smelled like Alaska, a fine smell, just different. I don't have to impose my bourgeois, Lower-48 teethism on this situation, I thought. It's just a dental disadvantage that he's negotiating rather resourcefully. Talk about making lemonade!

I can accept this situation and this person, I decided. I have the power to deem this *not* a grotesque horror show.

And I was right. Not and-now-Danny-and-I-are-married right or anything. But he did quietly put his teeth back in after he was finished with my foot, and we did get through breakfast fine, and then we waved and smiled hello in the bar for all of the four months until I moved back to Philadelphia for good.

BLIND DATE OFFENSE #88

Removal of any integral body part without warning

The Group Date

"Diane Arbus is overrated!"
Brian R., 19

BRIAN TOOK SEVERAL STABS at social groups his freshman year. He joined the college radio station and a fantasy baseball league and attended lectures on beat poetry and impeaching Bush. But he couldn't find his people. He always felt too sweaty and voluble at his small college in Maine. He wondered if a person could talk too much *and* be too passive.

He pursued girls so obliquely that they didn't notice. He fell hard for two freshwomen, Sarah, then Mai, his first semester. He took so long, however, to declare his intentions that platonic friendships had already formed.

He was grateful for Sarah and Mai's companionship, as he had great difficulty befriending men, too. At parties or in his classes, people would flutter to him when they found out he'd grown up in Manhattan, but then they would intuit his essential uncoolness and drift away. Sometimes he felt like bad PR for the city, like he was single-handedly erasing its mystique in the provinces.

Social hopes for second semester centered on his photography class. There was a lot of socializing built in and there were more women than men—mostly cute, geeky girls in thrift-store glasses. There was also a black guy and an Arab guy, which made the class his most diverse. For once, Brian the blue-eyed Jew was not the "ethnic" in the room.

Khalid, the black guy, was older, with long dreads and a fluid gait. Brian knew it was messed up to compare an African American to a lion, but he couldn't help it when Khalid rolled into the room. Brian had eavesdropped on Khalid's conversations with girls and had plotted an opening line for next Tuesday's class. He would debunk Diane Arbus. Khalid's pictures were better than anyone else's in the class, but Brian didn't want to open with anything as corny as a direct compliment.

But Brian never had to use his gambit. That Tuesday, at the beginning of class, Khalid wandered over and said, "Brian, right?"

"Yeah. Khalid?" As if he didn't know.

Khalid smiled gratefully at this like Brian was some celebrity who'd remembered him from an autograph signing. Brian basked—so little charm had come his way recently.

Khalid proceeded: "So I got a personal question for you."

"Sure. What's up?" Brian steeled himself.

"Are you single?"

"Single? Uh, yeah. Right now anyway. Why?"

Khalid scuffed his feet shyly. "My friend Meredith and I are helping each other out. I'm supposed to find her a cool guy and she's going to find me a cool girl, and then if you all are willing, we'll go on a double date."

Poor Brian didn't even get one second of happiness. Suspicion reared up instantly because nothing like this ever happened to him. Guys grokked his geekiness even quicker than women did. What was really going on? Did Khalid need an unthreatening wingman? How in the world could Khalid mistake him for "a cool guy"?

But Brian said that sounded great. He wasn't so much of a loser that he'd pass up opportunities out of his stupid fears—you had to give him that. He realized a bit too late that a true non-loser would have asked something about Meredith.

It didn't seem to matter. He was so happy punching Khalid's number into his cell phone and being punched into Khalid's in turn. A couple of days later, Khalid called to invite him to dinner at his apartment with Meredith and Roberta, the friend Meredith had procured for Khalid. It all sounded incredibly sophisticated to Brian. This would be his first dinner party.

Brian got to Khalid's house five minutes early and sat in the car for fifteen. He gave up on the girls arriving first and knocked. Khalid opened the door with an oven mitt, which he raised 90 degrees to soul-brother-shake height. Animal fat and garlic smells blasted deliciously from inside. Brian went in and watched him cook. He was overwhelmed by Khalid's masculine omnicompetence. His mind hurtled stupidly to and fro.

"Diane Arbus is overrated!" he finally blurted.

"You think? Hey, can you grab that potholder off the counter and put it on the table? My stew is ready."

Embarrassed, Brian rushed to help, and the doorbell rang. "Want to let in the ladies, bro?" Khalid asked, grabbing wineglasses and raising his eyebrows.

They were cute, especially the shorter one with the nose ring.

Brian breathed deep and opened the door to two nondescript white girls. They were cute, to be sure, especially the shorter one with the nose ring. He would have been happy to be naked with either one. But in this magical, fragrant kitchen with his new "bro"(!), he was struck first by Meredith and Roberta's similarity to the rest of the female student body. Poor Khalid must've been so bored in this Podunk town!

"Come in," he said. "I'm Brian. Khalid's cooking." He looked back and forth.

The taller one, his second choice, said hey, then called out, "Smells good, Khalid!" Meredith. Too bad. He turned to nose ring and said, "You're Roberta?" They walked back to the kitchen together. "Yeah." She dropped her voice, "I don't know why it didn't hit me how weird this whole thing is until tonight." Weird, yeah, but she never took her eyes off Khalid. She was obviously pleased with her draw.

"How do you know him?" Roberta asked.

"Photography class. He's really talented." Brian and Roberta gazed at Khalid for another moment, then jumped to help. Brian didn't actually exchange words with Meredith until they were seated across from each other, Khalid's stew ladled onto their plates.

"So Khalid tells me you're a good photographer," Meredith said politely after everyone had oohed and aahed over the food.

"Really?" Brian stole a happy look at Khalid, who nodded briskly. "That's nice of him to say, but really, he's the one. He blows everyone else in our class away." Brian and the girls looked around the room for photos on the walls, and then rushed over to admire them.

This was how the whole evening went. Khalid was a gracious host, praising Meredith and Brian, asking Roberta good questions. Whenever he turned his light on any of them individually, they felt fascinating. But when the light shone elsewhere, they could observe the scene more coolly. Brian and the girls understood that none of them were in Khalid's league. If not for the secondary glow, the "wonder what Khalid sees in him/her," Meredith and Brian might never have exchanged numbers.

After his first lackluster date with Meredith, Brian was longing to ask Khalid about her. Had Khalid and Meredith ever been involved? Was Khalid even aware that Meredith was in love with him? When he tried to ask him about how it was going with Roberta, Khalid was vague. "She's a cool girl" or "Yeah, she hit me up on Facebook the other day."

To Brian's joy, he and Khalid were hanging out and becoming friends. They went to movies together, watched college basketball games, talked about classes and books and girls, not just Meredith or Roberta.

Khalid was, not surprisingly, usually dodging women's advances. "Some of these farm girls have never even *seen* a black dude," he laughed, "and the wild ones all want to check that shit out." He had the kindness to act as though Brian shared this problem of excessive attractiveness. "She was macking on you, son," he'd say, and Brian would be thrilled despite knowing better.

Meredith soon hit Brian with the phrase he expected on his tombstone: "I think of you more as a friend." But unlike a lot of girls who wriggled out of his arms, she actually kept up the friendship.

Soon he realized why. She'd ask casually, "You seen Khalid lately?" The first few times, Brian said yeah, and Meredith proceeded to grill him: "Who was he with? How long did he stay? Has he mentioned me?" (Roberta did the same thing when he ran into her.) Khalid seemed to be phasing Meredith out of his life, almost as if to make room for Brian.

Soon Brian started lying to Meredith, telling her no, he hadn't seen Khalid. And then Meredith stopped answering his calls and texts.

It was sad, but only a little. As badly as he needed a girlfriend, his "bro" was the real prize of the double date.

The Poacher

The third wheel takes the helm

Hope M., 41

IT WAS MY FOUR THOUSANDTH or so Internet date, and I had learned the "coffee or a drink only" rule. There's nothing worse than knowing instantly that there's no chemistry and being locked into an entire meal. Maybe some people do online-date to make friends (frankly, I don't believe anyone who says that—who wants to be friends with someone who rejected them?), but I was after a husband.

Peter seemed quite promising, though, so I said yes to dinner. He had a good job, he'd been divorced for two and a half years, his profile said he wanted to get married again, and he'd only been online dating for a month. It's best to scoop them up before they're jaded— and I would know.

I admit it, I hate the process. The only thing that keeps me dragging myself out to these spouse interviews is that so many couples have met online. Plus, I work at a health care policy journal, and I don't meet single, straight men. If I don't Internet date, I don't date.

When I first saw him, I was glad I'd put aside the coffee/drinks rule. He was just the right level of good-looking—not terrifyingly out of my league, a little worn-looking, but attractive. He had strong forearms, one of my favorite body parts. I couldn't read what he thought of me. It's hard to tell interest from politeness when you don't know someone. The first—and in retrospect, last—good sign was when he ordered a bottle of wine with dinner. You don't do that with someone you want to escape from.

For the first twenty minutes, our questions seemed perfunctory, but then during our second glass of wine we found ourselves arguing animatedly over policy. I told him that holding out for single-payer health care was ridiculously pie-in-the-sky and he quoted insurance statistics at me. In case you can't tell, this was actually enjoyable, for me anyway. This was D.C., and he seemed engaged in the conversation.

"The question is whether any president could stand up to the insurance companies," said someone else. I whipped my head left and saw a pretty young Asian woman smiling at us from the next table. She was sitting right next to me, facing Peter. I widened my eyes at her rudeness and waited for him to point out that this was a private conversation.

"Exactly!" he said. "That's what I've been trying to tell Hope here, that with enough political will this could happen. Even the most conservative economists grant that health care does not follow market rules!"

The Asian woman appeared to be dining alone. She craftily took my side and said why she thought single-payer was a long shot. She continued her brilliant triangulation by reaching to shake my hand, not Peter's, and saying, "My name's Y-lang, I work for Congressman L_____," naming a famously liberal Representative.

> She craftily took my side and continued her brilliant triangulation by reaching to shake my hand.

Now would be the time to cut her out of the conversation, but I had no idea how to do so without looking bitchy. "Hope McManus," I muttered, resisting the urge to crush her tiny knuckles. Peter leaped out of his chair and shoved his beautiful forearm at her and introduced himself. They held the handshake longer than she had with me. As he sat back down, she scooted her chair closer to mine. At the same moment, he scooted closer to her. I ground my teeth.

We, or should I say, they, continued their stupid debate while I picked at my salad. Y-lang drifted closer and closer. As she was making a fascinating point about restructuring Medicaid payments, she actually stabbed her fork onto *my* plate and popped a piece of *my* asparagus into her mouth!

I had a brief hope that she'd stabbed herself in the foot. Helping herself to my food was so bizarre, so rude, that Peter was bound to be as shocked as I was.

So I looked right at him, for the first time since he'd spoken to her. I'd been afraid of what I'd see. But now I did see. The politeness-or-interest question was answered with painful clarity. His interest in her made his politeness toward me painfully clear.

If he'd even noticed the asparagus-poach, he seemed to have found it adorable. After riffing and laughing and teasing with her, he turned and asked my opinion as if including someone's grandmother in the conversation.

I was furious. And I was not going to make it easy for her. I had to pee, but I would not leave her alone with him for them to plot their next date. Her bill came first and she ignored it. When ours came, I watched to see how he was going to play this. If he let me pay for my half, he'd look cheap; if he picked up the whole thing, it'd look like a date.

Instead, he went to the bathroom, and she followed right behind! I sat there staring at the brown leather folder, imagining what he was telling her about me. Maybe how relieved he was that she turned up so the night wouldn't be a total waste.

My face burned. I looked at the three dirty plates, two empty wineglasses, and one bill, and then I walked out. Let her pay for my salad.

The Noodle Man

A comedy of (table) manners
Tina M., 40

A **FEW YEARS AGO,** I was writing a lot on my laptop in various cafés. Which of course meant a lot of peering over my laptop at everyone who walked into the café. While doing the latter, I dreamed up the perfect boyfriend: a schoolteacher who's also writing a novel. I gave him the teaching job so he wouldn't always be in the café, crowding me, but we'd still share writing. And when I did see him, he'd have good stories to tell me about the kids in his school.

I told my friend Jane about my epiphany, and she gasped. "I have him! I have your perfect guy! He's an English teacher in public high school and an unpublished novelist, single, forty-ish, attractive-ish, a good guy."

His name is Sean. Jane gives him my phone number and he calls up and suggests we meet at a good noodle place I know. He orders noodles, we talk, well, mostly he talks. But I like him okay. It could go either way at this point.

His meal comes and he commences to shovel a huge mouthful, seriously, about a third of the noodles from this giant bowl, into his mouth. He's interrupted his own sentence with this move, and I watch this waterfall of noodles cascading out of his mouth. I'm also silent, wondering how he gets out of this.

How he gets out of it: He lays down his spoon and brings both hands up to the noodles. He grabs two fistfuls, bites and lets the severed ends splash back into the bowl. Then he slowly struggles with the still-massive mouthful, swallowing and chewing with his cheeks distended like a squirrel's.

I politely give him the benefit of the doubt. It must have been an error of judgment. But he does the same thing again. After pulling the excess away from his mouth, he asks me, "So what's your favorite movie?" I say "Woody Allen's *Sleeper*. You?"

"*Tampopo*."

A few days later he calls for a second date, and I'm sick with a fever. Still, I decide to get it over with and tell him, "No, thanks, I don't think we clicked, but I'm flattered that you called, and good luck."

He answers indignantly, "What do you mean, no? I'm thirty-seven years old and nobody has *ever* turned me down for a second date before!" I hemmed and hawed, even told the truth that he talked too much, but he wouldn't hear any of it. Finally, I get him off the phone.

The next day Jane calls and demands to know why I turned Sean down. I tell her that he talks too much and added, "He also has an odd noodle habit." Jane seems as baffled as Sean did; she, too, believes in his irresistibility.

Two weeks after that, Jane reports back that some other friends were wondering why I hadn't gone out with him again. Jane told them that I'd mentioned noodle-eating, and they all exclaimed, "We *told* him to stop doing that, but he thinks it's sexy!"

BLIND DATE OFFENSE #22
Table manners that double as performance art

The Case for Short First Dates

The blonde time bomb

Rolf J., 65

I AM A GERMAN, sixty-five years old, married twice and twice divorced. My children are grown. I have my own business, which leaves me free to travel. A few years ago, when I was sixty-two, I read an advert in the London *Sunday Times* that said, "Attractive, blonde, slim, cultural, intelligent English lady living in the South of France looking for successful, good-looking, intelligent man to join her in her villa." I knew "successful" meant rich. Most women want money, but they say "successful."

I wrote and told her I knew her part of the world, as I had friends living near her villa. She wrote back and said, "Come visit when you're in France." She also sent me a photo. It was taken from a distance, but still,

she looked so good that I decided not to wait till
I visited my friends, and I booked a flight.

I told her my flight information and flew from
Munich to Montpellier. My plane was delayed two
hours, so I called her on my mobile phone to tell her.
She said, "Fine, call me when you get to the airport."
So I did, and I heard a dog barking and a male voice
in the background. She sounded flustered, annoyed.
She said, "Can I pick you up an hour from now?"

After a half-hour of waiting, I went to the pick-up
lane. It was a tiny airport, and there was only one
car there. I approached the driver's window and said,
"Excuse me, are you Miss X?" She barked at me, "Yes,
and where have you been!?!" I was half-an-hour early,
but did not want to argue as I did not want to be
stranded at the airport.

Her mood abruptly switched to friendliness once
I got in the car. She was chatting away, looking at
me, and touching my arm—so much, though, that she
stopped looking at the road and ran over the curb as
we left the airport. She drove off the road at one point,
to the very edge of an embankment. I was terrified.
She looked good, blonde and thin like her photo, sexy,
but nevertheless I was alarmed by her driving and her
erratic mood.

We got to the hotel, as planned, and she dropped
me off and said, "I'll see you tomorrow at 10 A.M."

The next morning I got to the lobby just before

10 to wait for her. At 11:30, a porter came to me and said, "Herr Jannings? A lady rang and she won't be here until late afternoon."

So I went swimming in the hotel pool and got myself a newspaper. I was reading it beside the pool when she finally showed up wearing a small sundress. In the daylight she looked ten years older, very thin. Her lipstick was smeared and her hands were dirty, black under the fingernails. But I thought, Don't judge a book by the cover, although the inside of the book had not seemed so good yet either!

She dropped down onto a beach chair beside me and said, "I could murder a drink! Gin and tonic, a lot of ice." I went into the bar to fetch it, but nobody was there, so I looked around the hotel for a bartender for fifteen minutes.

She drove off the road at one point, to the very edge of an embankment.

When I got back with her drink, I saw that she was angry. As soon as I handed her the glass, she reached into her drink, grabbed a handful of ice, and threw it at my face.

I was astounded, speechless. Then she grabbed my newspaper, and said, "I have to look for a job!" But the section she began to read was "Prospective Buyers of Villas." From behind the paper, she said, "I have to make a living, you know," then in the same barking tone, "So tell me about yourself."

So I told her about my business, but I soon realized she wasn't listening at all. She made a few notes on my paper and then said, "I have to go now." I walked her to her car. In the light I noticed that it was brand-new but had no side mirrors, a big dent in the side, and another dent in the back. She got into the car, rolled down the window, and gave me a big smile. "I'll call you later," she called out gaily. I never saw her again.

I stayed in the hotel for a week because my flight back was nonrefundable and my friends from the South of France were on holiday in Australia. I thought about trying the local personals to find a companion for the week, but couldn't bring myself to do it. I watched many movies on the hotel television instead.

The Tiny Purple Pimp

Video kills the radio voice

Monica K., 26

I WAS IN MY EARLY TWENTIES, going to med school in Cincinnati. I'd never really dated anyone seriously. To be honest, I was a virgin. One day I called a radio station to request "Purple Rain." The DJ and I chatted about Prince and how terrible the movie was, and he ended up asking me out. A DJ seemed like a celebrity to me, and of course he had a sexy voice, so I figured I'd go, for the adventure.

I was on the phone when he showed up at the door. I looked through the peephole and blurted out, "Good god!" to my friend. I'm five feet eleven inches tall and he was probably five feet five inches—and at least fifty years old. He had long blond hair. And he was wearing a purple velvet suit! He looked like a Muppet of a pimp. (I was in jeans and a sweater because he'd said "casual dinner.")

He drove around and around, playing the car radio way too loud, and it became clear that he had no idea where he was taking us to eat. Finally, he got us to a chicken wings bar downtown. His pimp outfit looked even more bizarre now, due to the fact that we were the only white people in the place. He looked like part of a minstrel show. I thought we were going to get beat up.

After devouring about forty-eight wings, he moist-toweletted his fingers and pulled a picture of a blonde woman from his wallet.

"She's beautiful, ain't she?" he asked me sadly. "We were married for twenty good years. And I had to go screw it up."

"How?" I asked politely, not wanting to know.

"We had a threesome with her best friend. My idea, of course. Things never were the same after that." I had never heard that word threesome before, but I figured it out from context. I had already wanted to go home, but now I *really* wanted to go home.

I told him I had an exam the next day. He drove me home and started looking for a place to park. I told him the parking places were always full and not to bother. But he found a place, parked, and went in for the kiss. I turned my head and he got hair instead, and then I leaped out of the car and ran to my door.

He kept calling for a month—had that been a good date for him?

Take My Wife, Please

The elephant in the two-door
Navah R., 51

YEARS AGO, I WAS LIVING and working on Long Island, not meeting men, so I went to a Jewish singles function at a community center. I went alone, like they say you should to be more accessible. After I spent an excruciating few moments standing outside pretending to look at the sky, a nice-looking man with sad eyes walked up and introduced himself.

He asked about my accent and I told him I grew up in Israel. This generally leads to a discussion of Middle East politics, which is fine, but not my favorite conversation: I live here now. David asked instead about what it was like to be an immigrant and did I like Long Island. I liked that, and soon we moved past interviewing and into real, un-self-conscious conversation. He seemed a little distracted, but nice, and interested in me.

A woman approached us as we talked, then stopped about ten feet behind him and glared at us. David saw me glancing over his shoulder and turned to look at her. He turned back and excused himself. They spoke in low, angry tones. She strode back into the hall and he walked to me, already shrugging defensively.

"Well, Navah, I guess this is the time to tell you my situation. I'm almost divorced, just a few i's left to dot. And I haven't quite closed on my house yet either. That woman is my ex-wife, almost, and right now I live in our basement. Her basement. What can I say? I'm here because the marriage has been over for a long time, and I hope you'll still see me again."

"You're both looking for people at the same mixer? Isn't that awkward?"

He laughed. "Of course it's awkward! And her car is in the shop, so now she's dependent on me for rides everywhere. When I told her I was coming here, she said, 'Well, if you can go look for someone new, I can too.' I've found it works better if I try to humor her."

"Who ended the marriage?" Her gaze at me seemed angry and I wondered if she still loved David.

"She asked for the divorce, but it was mutual."

"Yes, I would like to see you again."

David smiled and actually jumped in the air a little. I didn't have to wonder if he liked me. And better that a man in his late thirties is divorced than never married. Shows he can commit.

He called me at 9:10 the next morning at my job. "There's an Israeli-American night at a park tonight— food, music, art. Will you go with me?"

I sped home from work at five and dressed up for the date. It was a nice night, so I waited for him outside. A blue two-door Toyota pulled up, and the man looked a bit like David, but he wasn't alone. The car stopped in front of me, and David's ex-wife stepped out of the passenger seat and climbed into the backseat, leaving the door open.

MOTHER KNOWS BEST

LESSON #59

"If he doesn't walk between you and the curb, forget him."

David hurried over. "I'm so sorry. We'd talked about going to this before I met you, and I begged her not to come, but she insisted. She *is* the one who told me about this event, so I couldn't very well tell her no. Do you mind?"

Of course I minded. It felt very strange to get into the front seat. "Hello, I'm Navah," I said, leaning into the car. "Are you sure you won't sit up front? I don't mind the back."

"No, no," the wife, Barbara, said. "I'm fine back here. Just get in."

David pulled onto the highway and praised the nice weather. It felt too strange to ignore her, so I turned in my seat and asked her questions about her job, which

she answered curtly. Then she said, "Israel, huh?
I spent a summer on a kibbutz when I was seventeen.
I couldn't wait to get home."

"Oh, why is that?"

"No, offense, but Israelis are the worst. Aggressive,
rude, chauvinist. No wonder you moved here."

I allowed that Israeli men were a bit macho but
gently defended my country, thinking that would
end it.

But she kept railing against Israel for its rude men
and then for destabilizing the region and the whole
world. She didn't quite say the country had no right to
exist, but she came close. The ride felt hours-long, but
actually lasted twenty-five minutes. We parked and the
two of them dipped their heads into the trunk to get a
blanket. They kept physical space between them, but
familiarity was there in all their movements.

We spread the blanket in the grass in front of the
stage. David sat in the middle. The music began and
two songs in, Barbara said loudly, "This isn't what I
expected at all. Take me to Judy's house, David."

He turned to me. "Her friend Judy lives close by. I'll
be right back." And he left! I sat alone on the edge of
the big blanket. It grew dark. I had no idea where I was
and wondered how David would find me in the dark. If
he was even coming back. I looked around and couldn't
think of anything to do but wait. This was before cell
phones.

He came back with a lovely dinner and a bottle of wine. Something about him made me smile instead of yelling at him for the craziest date I'd ever been on. We laid down and looked at the stars after we ate. The music was lovely, we agreed. After the concert ended, we talked for a long time, lying on our sides. He didn't trash Barbara, so I didn't either; we just flowed around that elephant in the room.

We did, however, have to pick up the cranky elephant from Judy's. The three of us rode in silence, David's and mine contented, Barbara's unfathomable. We could not kiss goodnight, obviously, but he gave my hand a little squeeze before I got out of the car, holding the seat forward for Barbara to jump up front. I felt his touch until I went to sleep.

Our kids love that story. At the end, they always ask, "And after that, you *married* him?!" Even Barbara laughs about it now.

DÉJÀ VU

Ever feel like you just keep dating the same person again and again, in a slightly different form? Are they all, come to think of it, sarcastic or stubborn or shut down? Do your relationships all follow the same arc, from excitement to comfort to disillusion?

There's the human tendency to go for the familiar, sure, but there's also the sheer *volume* of dating we're doing these days. We now date enough to forget someone we've dated! (Thanks, Interweb.) When someone says, "I feel like I know you," they may indeed be right. Welcome to The Twilight Zone.

The Endless Spelling Bee

A case of Internet-dating amnesia

Aaron B., 30–34

I SWEAR TO GOD, this story has gone around so many times that it's actually been told to me by someone I didn't know.

I was about thirty when an old friend called and asked, "Are you still single? My girlfriend has a friend for you."

I called her up. We had a good phone conversation and decided to go out for dinner. Went to a nice place on the Upper West Side. I thought she was attractive, and the conversation was going okay. She brought up relationships, which led me to ask, "So how long *do* you have to date someone before you sleep with him?" She replied, "This is inappropriate for first-date conversation. Let's segue out of this." I said okay, sure.

Then she says, "By the way, do you know how to spell *segue*?" At this point in my life, I do not know. I say, "S-E-G-W-A-Y." She looks down as if in disgust, her head just falls in disappointment. I say, "What's the matter?"

She sighs and says, "I really need someone who's smart and intellectual, someone who reads *The New York Times.*" Then she spells *segue* for me.

I ask her to expand on her need for a *New York Times* reader. She says, "Like what do you do when you read the *Times* and you don't know a word?"

I joke, "I don't know, I probably sound it out, 'seg-you,' and try to figure out meaning from context."

She doesn't laugh. She stares at me hard and asks, "Do you know who Frank Lloyd Wright is?" And I'm embarrassed to admit that at this point in my life I didn't know, so I joke again and say that he's one of the brothers who invented the airplane, knowing he wasn't. Again with the disappointed head-drop.

So I try to joke again; I ask her, "Well, do you know who Art Vandelay is?" and she says, "No, who's that?" I explain that he's the architect George Costanza pretends to be. Blank look. "You know, *Seinfeld*?!" I slap the back of my hand into my other hand and say, "Come on now, keep up! How come you don't know this? I need pop culture."

She says, not smiling, "Sorry, I don't watch that show."

Soon after that, she made an excuse and left. She didn't even thank me for dinner.

A few weeks later, I'm bored and I call a bunch of friends and everyone's got a date or plans, so I dial this girl again—what the hell, she's cute. So she answers the phone and I say who I am and she greets me amazingly warmly: "Oh Aaron, it's so great to hear from you. How have you been? I hadn't heard from you and I was worried." I'm taken aback and try to figure it out. Maybe she realizes she was kind of a jerk and feels bad?

We go out a few days later. We're at dinner and she's staring at me really hard. She says, "Did I ask you how to spell *segue*?" I realize what a mistake it was to call her, and I decide to have fun, so I say "No."

"Are you sure?"

"Of course, I would remember that."

"Okay, so spell it."

"S-E-G-U-E," I reply.

"Can I ask you another question?"

"Sure."

"Do you know who Frank Lloyd Wright is?"

"He's the famous architect who did the Guggenheim. Doesn't pretty much everyone know that?"

She answers, "Well, I went on a date a few weeks ago with a guy who, get this, thought he was one of the Wright brothers who invented the airplane."

"Oh my god. What a tool. Who could think that?"

She took the bait: "I know! I never heard from that guy again."

We ate dinner, and that was that. (I let her pay her half.)

Three years later, I go on J-Date for the first time. I met a lot of liars, a lot of falsified pictures. Somebody sends me a wink—and it's her again! For such a towering intellectual, she sure has a crappy memory.

I couldn't resist. I replied to her wink with five letters: "S-E-G-U-E."

Rondelay of Misery

A therapeutic epidemic
Sharon C., 39

SHARON'S DATING EQUILIBRIUM was fine when she met Roland. She'd been on Nerve.com for a year and had adjusted to the rhythms of search, contact, e-mail, phone, hope, fantasy, and disappointment. She'd figured out how not to get emotionally flattened and how to bring a nugget home from each date—a visit to a new bar or neighborhood, new information about an unfamiliar profession or hobby or home country.

Roland was terse and decisive, which she liked. Her least favorite were the dilly-dalliers, the e-mail Cyranos going on and on. When she arrived at the bar, she sat next to him. "Hi, you must be Roland. I'm Sharon."

Roland glanced at her and went back to his half-empty glass. "Do you want a drink?" he asked without looking at her.

"Yeah. Mayb—"

"Well, then order one."

She did, and sat there wondering what to say. As she paid the bartender, Roland stood up, drained his glass, and slammed it on the bar. He took the quickest look at her, turned to the door, and said, "Enjoy your drink. I'm outta here."

And he was gone. It was shocking enough that Sharon barked a high little laugh. The bartender joined in, probably relieved that she hadn't cried and that he didn't have to pretend he hadn't witnessed the brutal exchange. "What an asshole" they exclaimed at the same time, and laughed more. He assured her that she'd dodged a bullet, that the guy'd seemed like a psycho the moment he sat down and demanded grain alcohol, neat.

This was comforting, and the psycho part was clearly true, but Sharon was thrown by the savagery. Were all her dates like that underneath, just better disguised? The truth of her year of online dating was that nobody had wanted her except the ones she didn't want.

She walked to her car. She'd driven forty-five minutes to meet this jerk, and now the freeway was packed. Staring at four lanes of brake lights flashing red, she considered the facts: She was coming up on forty in Los Angeles, an unenhanced, unskinny forty. And L.A. did not love its elders.

On the long drive home, Sharon resolved to henceforth look primarily for "kind" and "interested in me." She would eschew shallow criteria and would be nobody's Roland. Everyone would get a chance.

She would be sorely tested on her next few dates. The first one after Roland was Bill. He was quite pudgy, which she noted but did not condemn. He explained over dinner that his situation was complicated. He'd had a son with an old friend who'd asked him for his sperm. That had evolved to shared custody of the five-year-old boy, who lived with his mother in Palmdale, two hours north of L.A.

After that every-other-weekend pattern had been established, Bill had impregnated his next serious girlfriend, Brenda. He'd been crazy about Brenda and was devastated when she'd told him, seven months earlier, that she was pregnant—but through with him. She wanted to have the baby but wanted nothing to do with Bill.

As her pregnancy dragged on, however, Brenda relented and told Bill he could be half-time father after all, but without any romantic involvement with her. She was due in less than a month and lived in San Clemente, an hour south. Bill's solution was to move to Whittier, exactly halfway between his born and unborn children.

He answered Sharon's increasingly high-pitched questions. No, he hadn't moved yet, but there was nothing stopping him as he was out of work. "And the good thing is that Whittier is only forty-five minutes from where you live," he said cheerfully. "Because I'd really like to have two children of my own soon, and I know you're thirty-six [she'd shaved off two years on her profile] and won't want to wait much longer."

This was presumptuous, but it got worse. Assuming, apparently, that they'd be starting a family, Bill the Breeder filled her in on his background, asking nary a question about the future mother of his children. He told her about his past as a spy for both the U.S. and Britain, occasionally lapsing into a Madonna-esque fake British accent. None of it was remotely believable.

The Sound of Seduction

PICK-UP LINE #66

"I'm so drunk I see three of you. Can I kiss the middle one?"

Sharon was determined, however, to let him down kindly. So she nodded politely, kept her disbelief to herself, even made excuses for him in her head . . . until they got outside the restaurant. Bill grabbed her wrists, pushed them over her head, and pinned them to the restaurant wall. Pressing his big body onto hers, he kissed her hard on the mouth. She wriggled away and only then let fly the question she'd smothered all evening: "Are you fucking kidding me?" (Smothered because "he's sort of sweet, he's really into fatherhood, and the poor guy's been driving so much— that's probably why he's fat. . . .")

He wasn't kidding.

The next two men Sharon met online brought up their psychiatrists within the first half-hour, which to be fair is not *that* unusual in L.A. First was Hank, a terribly nervous pet groomer. Within the first ten minutes, Hank told her he was there on doctor's orders. "My therapist thought Internet dating would help treat my social disorder." She had never been deemed "treatment" on a first date.

> The next two men Sharon met online brought up their psychiatrists in the first half-hour.

Worse than the confession was his constantly dripping nose. For some reason, Hank took a long time to sniff it back in or wipe it with a Kleenex. Sharon found herself watching in suspense as the mucous descended, wondering how he could bear it.

But under the new acceptance plan, she overlooked the snot, and accepted a second date to see *Moulin Rouge*. During the movie, she glanced over just in time to see his tongue snake up and slurp in a long drip. She shuddered as she realized why he waited so long: The stuff was like *food* for him.

Perhaps the third man of the new regime would bring the charm. Hector was clearly sweet, excited to meet her, and smart—a computer programmer. Okay, he was a nerd, but nerds were acceptable. "Kind" and "interested" were her only regulations, with the new amendment "doesn't eat his own snot."

They met at an Indian restaurant, and she had

to remind herself of the no-discrimination policy. If
nerds were looking to file a class-action suit, Hector
would be the model plaintiff. Tall, skinny, weak chin,
thick glasses. His three topics of conversation were
Gregorian chants, comic books, and Harry Potter.

Sharon had read two of the Harry Potter books
and steered the conversation there. Hector grew very
animated on the topic of the relationship between
Harry and Dumbledore. She encouraged him with
questions and comments, and he pontificated joyfully.
Until he burst into tears.

"What's wrong?!" Sharon asked.

He sobbed, "I knew this would happen. I discussed
this with my therapist. I knew I'd come out and meet
you and I'd get too emotional."

Sharon murmured, "Oh that's all right" and maybe
even "There, there." She wasn't quite sure whether
something about Dumbledore had set him off, or if it
was just the fact of a woman being nice to him. Hector
regained his composure for about a minute, and then
he was off again. This time he ran to the bathroom and
stayed there for ten minutes. The waiter cleared the
plates, and Sharon asked for the check.

Hector emerged from the bathroom and slapped
his hand over the bill. "I've got that," he boomed in a
manly voice. Then he suggested they walk in the park
across from the restaurant. It had a maze painted onto
the concrete, and Hector joyfully skipped in. He ran

through the maze, staring down at his path with the concentration of a little kid. A kid who'd been sobbing inconsolably fifteen minutes earlier. Watching him, she thought about Bill the Breeder and how much work children were, how much work *people* were.

Hector looked up at Sharon and clapped his hands. "Don't you wish all life was like the maze and you could just get lost in it whenever you want?" She nodded wearily. "Sure I do, Hector." She pleaded an early morning and drove home.

He called around midnight to tell her he'd gotten one hundred pages into the new Harry Potter and to thank her for inspiring him. She let it, and his subsequent calls—seventeen in the next four days— go straight to voice mail.

Each time she heard his high, yearning voice enunciating his phone number and reporting his Harry Potter progress, she felt a little like Roland. Her equilibrium was gone. She had no idea what "giving someone a chance" meant beyond not storming out two minutes into the first date. How much chance was she supposed to give? She couldn't be everyone's consolation prize. She quit online dating for the rest of the summer and fall.

Po-Po a Go-Go

How a legend stays that way
Sheila O., 32

IF CRAIGSLIST AND ADULT FRIEND FINDER weren't anonymous, Sheila would be a legend. Some say she dates like a man, but only famous men score like she does. She "sleeps with" several new guys every month (quotation marks because she usually leaves before dawn). Among her gallery of sayings: "I don't believe in second dates."

Sheila's magnetic. She's big and loud and funny and restless and challenging—charismatic and a little scary. She processes alcohol like it's some mixture of coffee, multivitamins, food, sleep, and air—she gains energy as she drinks, and an ever-widening area around her becomes celebratory and reckless. A favorite among Boston bartenders despite her frequent spills, Sheila spends big and tips well.

Several booty-call regulars supplement her dates,

most of which are Internet-procured. One Tuesday she was finishing up at her job as a data analyst, looking forward to a date with a redheaded basketball fan she hooked up with every six months or so. He texted her that he was "2 tired sorry."

She fired off a female-seeking-male craigslist ad from her work computer: "Want to watch the Celtics game in a bar with me? Every time the Celtics block a shot, we'll DO a shot." She described herself as "fourth-generation Boston-Irish, wicked fun, not-plus-size-but-not-skinny—a shape the brothers seem to love." In five minutes, she got this e-mail: "Rocky's in Central Square? Halftime? U sound like a fun girl. –Mike."

They e-flirted, then she gave him her phone number and they texted their way to a plan. Mike was funny and loose. Sheila's not too fussy about looks, job, education or, obviously, romantic intentions. The only thing a man absolutely can't be is boring.

Mike texted "I'll be in uniform, OK w u?" Sheila asked what sort of uniform and Mike replied that he was an ice-cream man. "Sweet!" she typed back. "Not soft I hope."

Sheila took the subway from work, put on her lip gloss and strode into Rocky's. She looked around and saw no white uniform. She frowned and went to the bar. "Hey Gerry, black and tan and a shot of Jameson's."

He'd already poured them. "Evenin' Sheila."

Suddenly a police officer materialized at her side, and mumbled in a low, sexy voice, "Excuse me, miss, did you file the complaint about the too-soft . . . ice cream?"

A huge smile broke over her face. "Fuck me, you're a cop?! That is wicked hilarious." She punched his arm.

Mike shushed her and explained quietly that he was not off duty till midnight. So until then, he couldn't drink, not openly, anyway, and they couldn't actually be on a date, though they certainly could chat since they were, after all—he elbowed her ribs—old friends. "Gerry knows the drill," he whispered, "I'll settle up our tab after midnight."

Mike kept Sheila entertained all night. The deception was fun. Sheila sneaked him sips of her whiskey when the Celtics blocked two shots. He told her his funniest line-of-duty stories; and they discovered they'd gone to rival high schools. They began leaning into each other sneakily. Every time someone drew close, Sheila "covered" for Mike: "Officer, this man says I'm peeping at him, but is it my fault he doesn't have curtains?" or "In my country, a red light means speed up!"

Sheila mentioned she played poker. Mike glanced at his watch and said, "Remind me to tell you something at midnight." The plot was thickening! Sheila threw back a shot.

At midnight he put his arm around her. "Damn, I wish you didn't have a day job."

"Well, that doesn't start for . . ." She consulted her watch. "Nine more hours." Sheila's alcoholic chemistry includes the ability to crunch numbers on no sleep. Some of her fellow analysts understood that coming to work in yesterday's clothes meant she hadn't been home; others thought she was just being efficient by rewearing an outfit. "What's the plan?"

"Poker tournament out in Revere at midnight. Twenty-five-dollar buy-in, they usually get twenty or thirty people entering, and the top three all win money. We can take the subway there."

LESSON #33

"If her kids don't have the same last name, forget her."

"Poker tournament. At midnight. With a cop. In motherfuckin' Severe!" Sheila proclaimed, using the working-class neighborhood's nickname. "There's nothing I don't like about this plan," she said, taking his arm. "To Wonderland."

Revere is at the end of the Blue Line at the Wonderland station, where Mike had a uniform locker. He greeted some transit cops, and Sheila followed him into the locker. They made out while he changed, and her energy surged even higher. She was crackling when they entered the back room of the steak house where the tournament was held.

She played well, but Mike played well *and* got the cards. Sheila came in seventh out of thirty-two players and Mike won the whole thing. As they walked out with his $600, the sun was coming up. Sheila had lost no bounce; Mike looked weary.

"You live nearby?" she asked, pressing her body into his side.

"Yeah, about a ten-minute drive."

An awkward pause, but Sheila was undaunted.

"Well, are we going there?"

"Sure, though I gotta tell you, I don't have much of a sex drive."

Not the seduction speech she'd hoped for. Sheila looked at her watch: 6:20 A.M. There was no point in her going home to sleep for an hour or two.

"I'll be the judge of that," she declared. "Let's go."

Sadly, he was right. They fumbled, sighing, in the morning sun for a while, and while he dozed or pretended to, she dressed and tiptoed out. She took the subway back to the city and yawned through a gross, greasy breakfast at an all-night diner, then got to her desk an hour early.

By lunchtime, she had told four coworkers the story, ending "We totally hooked up, and I haven't been home." By the end of the day, she'd had a great time that morning.

Familydar

A very special game day
Dolores S., 71

IN 1982 I WAS LIVING out in Pennsylvania, and my youngest child, Kyle, had started his first year at the Naval Academy. His big sister, Melissa, had just graduated from U Penn and had a good job.

I was a little lost with no kids around, and I was really looking forward to driving into Philadelphia for the Army-Navy game. My friend Sue was always up for a trip, so we went together. Kyle wasn't even going to be there; Sue and I just decided to make a day of it.

Navy won, yay! Sue and I went to a bar in a hotel nearby to celebrate. A young man sat down next to me and we started talking. He was in his third year at West Point, and had actually played in the game. He was with an older man, maybe a cousin. I teased him about losing the game—I knew from Kyle what a terribly big rivalry that is. The young man, William, was so nice and I felt so comfortable with him.

I talked about Kyle. William told me that his mother had died when he was young, and my heart went out to him. Self-consciousness began to fall away. We told each other details of our lives, some intimate, while his cousin and my friend Sue talked. We were obviously very simpatico.

He suddenly asked if by any chance I had a daughter. I said, "Yes, as a matter of fact," and pulled out a picture of Melissa, who's a year older than William.

Melissa is a beautiful girl, and that was obvious from the photo. William asked me, formally, like a military boy, for permission to write her.

Melissa was involved with another man at the time, but William wrote that he would like to come meet her before Christmas. He said even if she wasn't available for dating, he'd hope to have a conversation with her like the one he'd had with me. I told Melissa that it was true, it was like we'd known each other for years.

> He suddenly asked if by any chance I had a daughter.

Their rendezvous was December 23, at my house. It was so obviously love at first sight; they just beamed at each other across my living room, until I "remembered" I had Christmas shopping to do, and left them alone.

Melissa soon broke up with her boyfriend and dated William until he graduated from West Point. Then (yup) she married him. They've moved all over the world, as he is still in the Army. They have three sons who are teenagers now. William and Kyle have become best of friends, too.

Those events of that day in 1982 were so unlike anything else I've ever done. I'm not the yenta type at all: William and Melissa are the only two people I've ever "set up" in my life. I'm certainly not in the habit of picking up sons-in-law, or any men, in bars. So I wonder, why did I chat up a young man in a bar this one time? Did I somehow know that William belonged in my family? How would I know that? It's still mysterious to me.

LET'S GO TO THE MOVIES

It's hard to know what a movie date means. I once blurted out, during an initial drink, "Let's go see such-and-such movie—it's playing *now!*" because I could not see generating another hour of conversation with the human before me. It was a good call: Movie, good; man, kind of pissy. But I've also dragged men I liked to movies I liked—to share an experience and more time together. The escape can be from or with.

In the latter case, a movie can let us fantasize side by side in the dark, performing some of the romance for us. But the tricky part is that we may be having totally different responses to what's up on the silver screen. Beware: The wrong movie can destroy a new and tender bond.

Il Presidente

A personal club, and why it should have stayed that way

Anthony A., 20

MY JUNIOR YEAR, I became president of the Italian Culture Club in order to get a key to my own private room at Brooklyn College. I got the key, but had to share the room with another club, the Italian Student Union.

I never thought anybody would actually join either of these clubs, but to my dismay they did. My private room was filling up with actual Italian club members, and one told me he was going to bring a nice single woman next time. I hadn't had a girlfriend in a long time—okay, ever—so I said sure.

This woman, I'll call her Luna, showed up a week later, on a Tuesday night, without the club member. In fact, nobody else was there; I'd hoped to get a paper written. She came in and said, "You must be Tony; it's so great to meet you. I love Italian culture, too!" She waved her arms around, "The food, the old buildings, *bellissima*!" She kissed her fingers and threw them up in the air.

She was good-looking and it was sort of a setup, so I didn't heed the first red flags she sent up, about fifteen minutes into our conversation. She said, "I feel my life is over and I'm only thirty-one, but maybe things will look up for me someday." It didn't take long for her to tell me her troubles: "I got laid off my job; my boyfriend wants to break up with me; the doctors removed a ten-pound cyst from my ovary; and I'm flat broke with my rent due."

I wasn't sure I believed everything she said. How does an ovary support a ten-pound cyst? I understand ovaries to be very small.

As day fell into night, I started to feel sorry for her. Her strange bug eyes had an empty stare. Her jerky and erratic body movements painted the portrait of a person who was not of sound mind.

She told me she was related to Stephen J. Cannell, the creator of *A-Team* and *21 Jump Street,* and that she'd met Robert Downey Jr. Even though we were on the third floor, Luna kept referring to the room as a basement. She seemed uncomfortable and nervous, and she never stopped talking.

I didn't know what to do; I felt like maybe I could help her before she did something crazy. "I'm normally quiet, but for some reason, today I feel I can tell you anything, Tony." Every ten minutes she would thank me for listening to her.

She wouldn't leave despite my hinting, so I suggested a movie. I'd rented *Boardinghouse,* a B-film about a haunted house filled with sexy women. It was one of the first films shot on video, and it is certainly ambitious. The big question is whether or not the film is bad on purpose. The director has claimed that to be the case, but I find it hard to believe.

> She wouldn't leave despite my hinting, so I suggested a movie. The film was an incoherent mess.

The film was an incoherent mess, much like my never-ending evening.

Around 9:30 P.M., the president of the other club showed up, a guy named Salvatore who never shut up. He was in his late forties. He entered the dark room and acted like he'd just walked in on two people watching a porno on the couch. Poor-quality slasher flicks do kind of look like pornos, minus the nude scenes.

"I'll be out of you kids' way in about ten minutes!" Salvatore took his usual seat and started jabbering. I spaced out and then heard him say, "My wife was two-timing me, then she told me, after my nervous breakdown no less, that I had to sleep in the garage. That's when I stopped living for others and started living for Sal. I got a divorce from my wife and started dating women who accepted me for me. I mean I broke up with a woman because she told me to use

conditioner in my hair. I told her I hate conditioner—
it feels like someone came in my hand—and I told her
good-bye."

There was no end in sight for this night. I never
knew this stuff about Salvatore, and Luna was
engrossed in every word coming out of his saliva-
filled mouth. "Now you guys know Salvatore, and
Salvatore knows a lot of people. I can help you look for
apartments, jobs, and that kind of shit."

"It's almost one o'clock. I have work in the
morning." I groaned at Salvatore as he searched
the Internet for photos of his daughter. That hint
went right over his head. I should have gotten up
and left but it was like watching a train wreck (or
Boardinghouse).

Finally Luna was ready to go, and I walked her to
the train station. "Thank you, Tony, for a wonderful
weekend," she said warmly. It was Tuesday.

A Greaser on Silk Stocking Row

A good girl's brush with the wild side
Linda L., 72

I **DIDN'T KNOW TILL I WAS IN COLLEGE** that my father had grown up poor. When I was seven, he was made president of the bank, which had "branches throughout the South." I didn't know what a branch was—I'd always pictured a tree on the bank's lawn—but I knew that those branches were important to our family. Those branches had to do with the fact that we'd moved from a big house in Alabama to a huge house in St. Louis and started going to the pool at the country club. Daddy became president of the Chamber of Commerce, and there were lots of big dinners with men giving speeches.

I thought my daddy hung the moon. I got in a fight with Peggy Gunson in the fifth grade when she denied that my father outranked Harry Truman.

"But my daddy's president of two things!" I shouted into her ignorant face.

My older brother and I went to a small private high school where everyone knew each other's families. I only dated boys from school; it wouldn't have occurred to me, to any of us, to date public school boys. All of us were going to college, many to Ivy League schools, and we liked our milieu. We may have sneaked a cigarette or a drink or a necking session here and there, but nobody wanted to rebel against the dress code or any of our parents' expectations. I hoped very much to have a life like Mother's.

I made my debut in 1954, the summer before senior year, and so did many of my friends. There were balls and cotillions, and golf and swimming parties at the country club. It was a glorious summer.

But the very next year, right after I graduated, Daddy got transferred to Decatur, Alabama, to start a new sector of the bank. I was heartbroken. I missed my friends terribly, and Decatur seemed small and provincial. It was also strange to see more of my Uncle Elmore, Daddy's brother. He and his family lived outside Decatur, in the same neighborhood as our maid. Daddy avoided visiting them and they didn't seem to like coming to where we lived, on a wealthy street known as "Silk Stocking Row."

I was so bored that summer. I knew only one girl in town: Susan, whose father was a colleague of Daddy's.

When I complained to her that I had no parties to go to and no beaux to date, her boyfriend suggested I meet a single boy he knew named Billy Joe. I gratefully said yes to the blind date, my first, and we arranged for him to take me to the movies.

Mother and Daddy were out at a party, and my brother was working, so I got ready by myself. I hummed along to Nat King Cole while I set my hair and ironed my blouse. I looked nice, and I was excited to meet my date.

The doorbell rang. I opened the door and beheld Billy Joe. His black hair was long and oily and sculpted into a pompadour. He had on a tight white T-shirt, with a pack of cigarettes rolled up in one sleeve. I half-expected to see a tattoo! He wore jeans and cowboy boots, and he slouched on my front porch. "Hah thay-er" he drawled. "Yew mus be Leein-da."

The Sound of Seduction

PICK-UP LINE #122

"You live on the nicest street; I've always wanted to see the inside of one of these houses."

He was a hood! A greaser! I had only seen people like this in movies. I never imagined anyone actually carried his cigarettes in his sleeve. My first emotion was panic—Mother and Daddy would see this creature on the porch—but then I remembered they were gone, thank God. I stared at him, not knowing what to say.

I didn't know people like this, and that was fine with me, thank you very much.

I suppose that sounds awfully snobbish, but all I can say is I'd been very sheltered. My dream date at the time was someone like Rock Hudson, a man who'd be comfortable at an elegant party. I knew some girls liked James Dean and Elvis Presley, but I thought they were crude and gross. Everything in my upbringing had taught me to avoid people like this Billy Joe.

But I had said yes, to Susan and to him, so I followed him down our circular drive to the street. He opened the passenger door of a beat-up Chevy convertible with some cheap plastic thing hanging off the rearview mirror. The car wasn't even clean! I assumed we were going to the movie palace in town, but he took off for the drive-in. "Ah thought we'd see a duh-bul feachah," he told me. "*The Grapes uh Wrath* and *Tobacco Road.*"

I wanted to flee more than ever. Didn't he know dates were supposed to be light and fun and gay? Why did I have to watch two depressing movies with a tacky boy in a greasy car? Maybe the girls in his neighborhood thought that sounded like a good time, but I didn't.

Plus, there was, of course, the reputation of drive-ins as a place for necking. I knew we'd get nowhere near that; I had already scrunched myself up against the passenger side door (boys called girls who did that "damn door-huggers"). I wasn't afraid that he'd get fresh with me; it was clear to both of us that Billy Joe would never cross the line that separated our worlds. He was, in fact, very respectful, asking me the whole time if I wanted another Coke or some popcorn, and what did I think about the acting and the story.

It was a different time. It didn't occur to me that it would have been scary for Billy Joe to come to Silk Stocking Row. Boys were in the driver's seat in the 1950s; we girls only reacted. All we could do was pull back with varying degrees of conviction—and with Billy Joe I fully meant it! The whole long date was tiring the way sharing a small seat on a bus is tiring: We were adjacent but I had to keep us apart.

I couldn't wait to get home and take a bath. After I toweled off and baby-powdered, I got into bed with my college brochures. I studied the pictures of the well-dressed, successful boys and girls on the pretty green campuses until I fell asleep.

Leaving Ice-Cold Las Vegas

First the gas, then the heat

Gabriel N., 43

I FIGURED MY CHIROPRACTOR'S RECEPTIONIST had a crush on me. Because it's weird to ask a back-pain client if he's single, right?

I'm feeling out whether she's flirting with me, so I go, "Who wants to know?" She giggles and says she's married, but that her friend Eileen is really great and for some reason she thinks we'll like each other. Eileen's a personal trainer and works long hours; she doesn't have time to go out and meet people.

"A lot of guys are intimidated by her looks," the receptionist adds. I figure what the hell.

I call her and we agree to see *The Usual Suspects.* She tells me where it's playing and we plan to meet there fifteen minutes before showtime. As I'm standing out in the freezing cold waiting for her, I see that she's gotten it wrong—*Leaving Las Vegas* is playing, not *The Usual Suspects*.

A blonde woman runs up to me waving her arms and babbling. "I think there's a gas leak and I'm worried about my cats. Do you mind dashing by my place? It won't take long; we can catch a later movie. Oh look, it's not *The Usual Suspects*! Huh, that's weird. Anyway, I really am not going to be able to relax till I check on my cats, so do you mind?"

She turns out to live seventeen blocks away. It is very cold. We walk to her place, wind blasting in our faces, to check on the cats. It turns out she doesn't even have gas heat, she has oil. False alarm.

We head back out into the ice and go to a Chinese restaurant. She is very pretty, so I try to shrug off my annoyance. But she continues to chatter in a sort of stream-of-consciousness way, and none of it sounds plausible. She'd been wrong about the movie, wrong about the gas; she seems to just assert things regardless of their veracity. The more I realize that she might be unhinged, the less I want to see her naked. (I guess that's just not my kink.)

She turns out to live seventeen blocks away. It is very cold.

Having understood that this date is going nowhere, I suggest we go see *Leaving Las Vegas*. Back at the theater, the ticket seller says the heat has just gone off.

"It just now went off? So it's still warm?" I ask. Yes, says the ticket seller. Good enough. In we go, to watch one of the world's most depressing movies. The theater gradually gets colder until, by the end, we're freezing to death again, just as we were at the beginning of our date. We walk to the subway, and she shakes her head. "What a disaster!" It was the first accurate thing I'd heard her say.

BLIND DATE OFFENSE #5
Recounting the entire plot of any movie

Crash

(went the date . . .)
Becky L., 38

BACK IN THE '90S, I met a guy through a very early version of the online personals. In those days it was normal not to post a photo. I loved his profile, and we had a great first phone conversation. Movies connected us, and because he also liked Jane Campion, Pedro Almodovar, and Luis Buñuel, I concluded that he was the male me, my soul mate.

Alan and I agreed to meet at a café and maybe go to a movie if we were both into it. (And obviously we both would be.)

I arrived first and looked at the menu. When he walked through the door I knew two things immediately:

1. That's him, and

2. There's no way I'd ever be interested in him as a boyfriend.

But the soup was good, and once I'd adjusted to my disappointment, we went back to the same enjoyable movie discussion our phone-selves had had. So when Alan asked about moving on to the next part of the date, I said, "Sure, let's go."

Two movies were playing on that block, in theaters across the street from each other: *Kama Sutra* and *Crash*. All I knew about *Crash* was that David Cronenberg made it and Holly Hunter was in it—I deliberately hadn't read reviews because I wanted to experience the new Cronenberg as purely as possible. Alan loved Cronenberg as well.

I also wanted to see *Kama Sutra,* but that would be a mistake, right? It had to be full of sex, so *Crash* it was.

> We went back to the same enjoyable movie discussion our phone-selves had had.

As the lights dimmed, Alan reached across the armrest and tried to take my hand. *Argh.* What could I do? Rather than pull away, I whispered, "I don't really feel like holding hands right now." I could feel his anger pulsing at my right side, building through the previews.

The film's opening scene featured graphic sex up against an airplane. Yes, I chose a movie that was all about people who are sexually stimulated by car crashes, and the characters let us know this by having sex pretty much nonstop. I was loving the movie, the cinematography was fabulous, the characters great, the study of obsession fascinating—but next to me was this man I wasn't attracted to, nursing his rejected hand and seething, and possibly getting turned on.

I got my punishment outside the theater. I was trying to escape in a flurry of pleasantries and film discussion, but he set his jaw and said accusingly, "Just tell me this. Why did you act as if you were available if you weren't?"

I almost cried out, "I was just trying to be nice and maybe make a movie friend!" Instead I mumbled an apology and slunk away, trying to leave him with a little moral victory.

Later I realized I'd made the classic rookie mistake. Our shared movie tastes had become, in my mind, the basis for perfect compatibility. A common pitfall of online dating—you mistake one good part for the whole.

E-Dissonance

A lesson in nutrition, balance, and grooming
Jared G., 22

I DIDN'T KNOW MUCH about dating sites, so I signed up on eHarmony my senior year. I assumed it was the best one, probably because it had the most ads. Now I know better.

The site sent me two matches around the same time: Brenda in New Jersey and Tiffany in Yonkers, where I lived.

Brenda was more responsive, but her e-mails made me think something wasn't right. I couldn't discern a personality there, and I didn't understand her life. Sometimes I would call her and a girl would pick up and either tell me I had the wrong number or that Brenda was sleeping. Brenda told me at some point in our second month of infrequent e-mails that her last relationship, five years long, had been with a woman. So there was that.

Tiffany was a little flaky, but I pursued her harder. Whenever that didn't seem to be going in a good direction, I would call Brenda to make myself feel better. It was skuzzy, I know.

One weekend Tiffany dissed me, while Brenda read my B-movie blog and even left a comment. I had some extra cash and I owed Brenda a chance, as I'd canceled plans with her a couple times. Maybe I would have a good time. . . . I got on a train to New Jersey.

MOTHER KNOWS BEST

LESSON #7

"Feminist, schmeminist. If he likes you, he should pay."

As the train pulled in, I saw her on the platform. She was a little bigger than her picture had allowed, but I'm big so that really wasn't an issue. We got in her car and she drove us to a Mexican restaurant. Everything sounded so good that I ordered a little too much food—appetizers and a huge main course. Before our order even got to us, we'd already eaten two baskets of free chips and salsa.

The first appetizer arrived, a make-your-own fajita-type dish with onions, cheese, and chicken. It came with three pieces of flat bread. Brenda's face fell. "What a shame there are only three pieces of bread," she said mournfully.

I said the only thing a person could say: "Don't worry, you take the third." "Okay," she said.

The entrées were on huge pastel plates with cheese and sour cream flowing to their edges. I couldn't finish mine, but Brenda finished hers. I was so full that I sneaked my hand down and unbuttoned the top button of my pants just as the waiter arrived with a dessert menu. I pulled my hand up to wave him away, but Brenda waved him back and ordered flan. I couldn't believe she was still going.

We drove to a strip mall to see the Al Pacino vehicle *88 Minutes.* On our way to the seats, she tripped on a tiny step and tumbled back into the aisle. She laid on her back clutching her knee and moaning. Everybody was looking.

I pulled her up to her feet. The previews were starting. "I think I need to go to the doctor," she gasped. I tried not to sound impatient. "Do you need me to drive you?" I wouldn't have minded so much if I'd known then that *88 Minutes* is perhaps the worst movie Pacino ever made.

She gingerly put her weight on the "injured" leg and smiled bravely. "I think I'll be all right, let's watch the movie." So we did, but she gasped and grimaced and grabbed her leg every time she shifted in her seat. When the credits rolled, she took deep breaths to prepare herself for the ordeal of standing up and walking out.

I assumed that, what with the injury, she'd want to get home, but she suggested we go have coffee and discuss the movie. Once we got to the coffeehouse, however, she didn't say anything about that or any other movie. Instead she returned to the topic of the "accident," which seemed to have grown in her mind to this terrible plummet.

Maybe reliving the horror got to her. She started to pull at a hairy mole on her neck. A hairy. Mole. She grabbed the hair with her fingernail and pulled. She rotated and craned her neck up at me and asked, "Did I get it?" (She hadn't.)

The date ended with her driving me to the train station. We waited for my train. As soon as I heard its rumble, I leaped out of her car without saying "I'll call you" or even "Great to meet you." She continued to I.M. me afterward and I ignored her for a while. Eventually I accepted one of her I.M.s; she asked if she'd done anything wrong on our date. I lied: "No, I was having personal problems and took some time for myself. Don't take it personally."

I felt bad. But really, it's *not* so hard to not pick a mole on a date. I even wonder if the girl was all there.

Hey, Small Spender

The real price of a matinee

Kevin O., 34

ABOUT TEN YEARS AGO, I answered a personal ad in the back of a gay magazine. I talked to the guy on the phone and we decided to meet for coffee and then go to a discount movie. We discussed how this was the last matinee in New York, still $2 for the first show, and how great that was.

At the coffee shop, I ordered coffee and a muffin, and my date, let's call him McDuck, ordered tap water. I offered him a bit of muffin and he took it, then another bite, then asked for a sip of my coffee.

We walked to the movie theater. The sign said, "Matinee, $3."

"What?" McDuck screeched at the ticket taker. "When did it go up?" "A month ago," said the kid in the booth. McDuck turned to me and asked if he could borrow a dollar, because he only has two bucks on him. O-kaaaay.

When we sat down (needless to say, without popcorn), he left an empty seat between us. And then, when the movie was over, instead of walking out with me, he told me he was going to stay and sneak into another movie at the same theater!

I have to hand it to him—between the two movies, the water in the coffee place (not to mention my muffin and coffee), he got a lot of date for his two dollars!

The Actress

She wasn't quite ready for her close-up
Steve R., 49

MY FRIEND EARL SET ME UP with this actress a couple years ago. I'd been back in my hometown of New Orleans for less than a year, following my divorce. So I asked around for a good restaurant to take her to. My cousin came up with this Korean place—that was still pretty exotic in New Orleans.

Earl had gone on and on about how great-looking this girl was. I kept expectations low, because, generally speaking, Earl talks a lot of shit. But not this time.

I picked her up at her house, and I couldn't believe what answered the door. She really did look like a movie star—long blonde hair, beautiful face. And she wasn't too skinny, like most actresses and New York City women; she had a butt like two bulldogs in a sack.

Janet didn't just look like a sexy angel, she also seemed to want me to like her. This was another nice change. New York City women start out pissed off; you're always digging your way out of a hole that you don't remember falling into. Janet, however, laughed at my jokes and seemed interested in what I had to say.

So interested that I ran off at the mouth during dinner; those big-ass bottles of Korean beer might have had something to do with it. My divorce had just been finalized. Janet kept asking questions. I tried to ask her about being in plays and movies, but she kept turning it back to me.

Before I realized it, I was telling her the story of my marriage falling apart. It wasn't a line to get her to feel sorry for me or anything—I just found myself opening up to this woman because she was nice, and because I hadn't told anyone the whole story.

> You're always digging your way out of a hole that you don't remember falling into.

"You're sure this isn't boring?" I asked her, and she said, "No, not at all, it sounds really painful. I'm sorry."

"Thanks," I said. "It was, it is, really painful. And I think I first knew it was over but didn't admit it when my mother was dying of cancer and Lila just fucking checked out emotionally. It was Not Her Problem." Saying the words to this sweet woman, sorrow overcame me as I remembered the trial of my mother's deterioration and the loneliness I felt when my wife withdrew.

I choked back a sob and looked down to hide it. "The day the doctor told me and my sister that our mom only had a few months was maybe the worst day of my life." I got a hold of myself and then finally looked up.

Janet's head was down, her arm muscles working minutely. She was texting under the table.

I was shocked sober and stared till she looked up.

"I'm sorry, what?" Her face was blank.

"Um, I was telling you about my mother's death? It was a pretty sad time for me?"

Janet snapped her phone shut and dropped it into her purse. "I'm sorry, Steve; I'm expecting an important call. Why don't you tell me again?"

She did this weird thing with the muscles in her face—she let them go slack, then pulled them up and back. It reminded me of an Olympic diver flexing at the end of the board.

"What do you mean tell you again?"

She furrowed her brow and found her "concerned" expression. "About your mom. How did she die? What kind of cancer?"

"Ovarian," I said with my eyes narrowed.

"And you loved her very much?" Her voice was huskier, her eyes watering.

"Yes, I did."

Janet pushed her lips together and then up in pity. From each of her big blue eyes fell two tears, but she never stopped gazing at me. "I'm so sorry," she said, shaking her head sideways and at me. She put her hand on top of mine. I was in a Korean restaurant, but I was really in a goddamn acting class. It was some *Twilight Zone* shit.

I called for the check that instant and took Janet home. She played the ride home "quiet and sad," much different from the friendly girl I'd driven to the restaurant. "I had a nice time," she said as she got out of the car. Driving home, I doubted everybody who'd ever said that to me.

BLIND DATE OFFENSE #98
Pretending to listen to your date while instead watching the game on a bar TV

HONESTY

I was amazed when I first heard that some Internet daters dismiss the other person during the date. They just say, upon parting, "Sorry, I'm afraid this isn't a match," maybe with a firm handshake. Or "There's no chemistry here" or "I don't feel a spark." (Even the most articulate people sink to these clichés during the insta-dump, making the whole thing that much squirmier.)

As a rejecter, I don't have the heart or the guts for that. And as a rejectee, I don't want it. An e-mail or phone call would be fine. Not returning my e-mail or call would be rude but still preferable to face-to-face rejection, especially with explanation, from someone I just met.

The other extreme—a liar—is of course worse. I'll take the brutally honest guy over the smoothie with his wedding ring in his pocket. But liars do make for good stories.

Drive-By

A parking-lot quickie
Helen D., 46

IT WAS A *BOSTON PHOENIX* AD. I was standing outside the pub where we were to meet. This (suburban) guy drives up and leans out the window. His voice was squeaky with anxiety and not-wanting-to-be-doing-this: "Are you Helen? The traffic is terrible. I can't find anywhere to park!"

I yell back, suggesting that he try a couple of blocks away. He says he will go around the block. A few minutes later he's back, shouting out the car window, "I can't find parking, and I'm not attracted to you!" Then he sped off, back to the suburbs.

The Truth Experiment

A good idea at the time

Francine P., 42

I'D BEEN DOING A LOT OF INTERNET DATING and was very frustrated. It seemed booby-trapped somehow—two friends had told me stories about online dates that went nowhere until they ran into the guys a year later in real life and began dating. It seemed like this technology designed to bring people together actually made it harder to get involved, and I couldn't figure out why or what to do about it.

These things were on my mind when I met Wilson; as was Michael Jackson, who had died the day before. At our rendezvous, my first impression of Wilson was that he was not as cute as his picture. (Why oh why don't people use realistic, maybe even unflattering pictures?) I was open to any other charms Wilson might possess, but I can't lie—looks do matter.

He was bright and we had enough in common to keep a conversation going. But he was trying too hard. I wanted him to relax.

Wilson sensed he was losing me, I think, and he blurted, "Don't you hate these things?"

"What things?" I asked, though I was pretty sure what he meant.

"Internet dates! You're never really present because you're always wondering 'What's she thinking?' Can I make a proposal?"

"I'm not getting engaged on the first date, Wilson."

> He was trying too hard. I wanted him to relax.

"She's funny, too. My proposal is that we tell the truth. Let's say what we're really thinking."

The notion provoked some anxiety, but also some relief. And curiosity.

"Okay," I said. "But let's keep talking about Michael Jackson because honestly, I was enjoying that conversation. You reminded me of three songs I'd forgotten. So yeah, let's tell the truth, but let's not go straight to couples therapy."

"Excellent. I was thinking the same thing. Really!" He smiled at me, too long. "Do you remember the video for 'Black and White' with all the morphing faces at the end? That terrified me as a child." Wilson was a few years younger than me.

"That was amazing!" I said. "And those dancing

aborigines and Indians with the horses circling
around them!"

We chattered on about music and race and
celebrity and plastic surgery and all those topics
Michael leads one to. Then, after the waiter cleared
our plates, Wilson said, "I'm thinking I want to kiss
you now."

Hmmm. My truth was that I had no desire to kiss
him. Would he want me to say that? Or did he propose
the game assuming that the only truth I could possibly
hide was my passion for him?

I sighed. I'd agreed to the game, so: "Wilson, I like
you, but I don't feel any chemistry." I looked down
while I said it, to give him privacy to absorb the blow.
I heard nothing, so I sneaked a look.

He was smiling and shaking his head, as if amused
by my naiveté. He leaned forward and explained,
"Francine, women don't care about that."

The truth that popped into my head was: This one
does! But once the little flash of indignation passed,
I realized I didn't want to squabble with this guy. He
didn't really want to know what I was thinking; he
just wanted me to like him. I suddenly sagged, as I so
often do on Internet dates, under the weight of human
beings' appalling vulnerability.

But I had to say something. Jack Nicholson
snarling, "You can't handle the truth!" popped into my
head and I smiled.

Wilson smiled back and took my hand. "Right? I mean, this—" he pointed at me and himself several times quickly, miming our bond, "what we have going here, that *is* chemistry."

Again with the helpful explanations of my thoughts. I turned the conversation back to the Jackson Five. At the end of the night, when Wilson went to kiss me again, I turned my head and gave him cheek.

When he e-mailed for a second date, I firmly but politely turned him down, giving no reason. He hit me with this: "Fine. There are plenty of women for me, but good luck finding a man at your age."

Thanks, asshole. Your "truth" just set me free.

The Glass-by-Glass Menagerie

Oh, just one more thing

Harvey P., 44

I'M CRUISING MATCH.COM one night and find this woman who looks great: forty, divorced, no kids, good job, pretty smile. I write to her, we flirt on e-mail, and we set up a date in a bar.

After she finishes her first drink, she says, "I have a confession." I have a good guess what it is—she looks older than forty. But she surprises me. "I actually do have a child. A son." Okay, weird lie, but whatever. I don't mind kids.

After the second drink, she's smiling a little bigger and waving her hands around more. "Alright, Harvey," she says, "I can't lie to you anymore. I actually have two kids, a boy and a girl."

During her third drink, she starts initiating body contact, laying her hand on my arm to make a point, brushing against my leg when she gets up to go to the bathroom. As she drains her glass, she says, "You know what, Harvey, I like you. So full disclosure this time. Harvey, I got three kids. My little girl Roseanne just turned five."

I did not stick around for drink number four.

BLIND DATE OFFENSE #51
Adjusting a lie more than three times

Do You Take This Woman, Man?

When pragmatism was the only way to shock
Lowell M., now 67

THE STRANGEST BLIND DATE I've ever been on happened, good Lord, more than forty years ago. Meaning two things: It was really strange, and goddamn, am I old!

It was 1967, and I'd landed in San Francisco after a stint in the merchant marine. Everyone's seen that '60s documentary stock footage so many times that it's been drained of all meaning. It's hard to convey that it really did feel like a revolution or a great social experiment—how thrilling it was to be young there and then. But believe me, it did and it was, and it could turn your head.

I rented part of a warehouse, bought a camera, and started taking pictures. After I tried LSD, I branched out into painting so I could document my hallucinations. A curly-haired girl named Sherrie made macramé plant hangers in another corner of the warehouse. We got to talking, and she was fascinated by my being from Nebraska and having been in the merchant marine. "A real American!" she kept saying. She told me she believed we were transforming society and that the death of all hang-ups couldn't be far behind. It sounds so silly now, with corporations even more powerful than they were then, but I was grateful to her for voicing what I'd been feeling: Anything was possible.

She lived with Dave, her "old man." (Ha! Now he really is!) The three of us took two great acid trips together in the redwoods. I liked tripping with friends much better than tripping alone, though it was kind of a drag when they'd go off to have sex. Soon after the second trip, they invited me to a dinner party. "There's a Swedish chick we want you to meet," Sherrie said, and Dave winked and outlined a curvy hourglass with his hands.

I'd never been to their apartment before. I climbed three sets of outdoor steps and entered a big, bright yellow room that held not one but two (two!) Swedish girls leaning their elbows on their knees atop an Indian-print couch. Ferns hung in little macramé hammocks all around them, and paintings dotted the yellow walls. Sherrie gave me a mug of sangria and introduced the tall girl as Hannah and the small

one as Renata. I was momentarily thrown off by lady
overload, so I walked away to look at the art.

I stopped at a painting that reminded me of a
Maxfield Parrish. A nude woman gazed out over
a gauzy fairy landscape. At the bottom, a touch of
whimsy: Her butt cheeks were separated by a rip in
the canvas. I laughed, and the girls
hoisted themselves up off the couch
to have a look, clumping over in their
white platform shoes. I checked them
out as they approached.

> I was momentarily
> thrown off by
> lady overload,
> so I walked away
> to look at the art.

Hannah was about six feet tall,
with a lot of makeup and high, stiff
blonde hair and, as Dave had suggested, major curves.
Renata was tiny, with huge dark eyes peering out from
underneath floppy bangs. When they drew near, I
pointed out the rip; the Swedes leaned in.

Renata laughed, but Hannah didn't. "You should
tell the person you bought this from that it's damaged,"
Hannah said to Sherrie as she straightened up. She
had a slight accent. "You should get money back."

Sherrie laughed, "I found it on the street, Hannah!"

We sat down at the table, and Sherrie pushed me
into a chair next to Hannah. Then she brought out
more sangria and a couple of joints.

I figured out that Hannah was "for me"—I'm six
five, so I always get the tall one. But I preferred small,
birdlike Renata, who laughed at the butt rip and said

she read tarot cards. I changed seats to get next to her and asked for a reading. She looked uncomfortably at the others, who nodded. She flipped the cards quickly and pronounced me generous and unconventional.

In a loud, almost theatrical voice, Hannah asked Dave and Sherrie if they were married. Dave, also sounding rehearsed, boomed back, "No, Sherrie and I think marriage kills brotherly love and community. The Man wants to divide us into family units and turn us all against each other."

Sherrie chimed in, "It's completely meaningless. We don't need the government in our bed." She ruffled Dave's hair.

I had turned Renata's chair around so I could massage her shoulders and her pretty neck. I was pleasantly stoned, wondering how to get her away from the rest of them. I felt her relax into my hands for just a moment, but then she leaped up and addressed the room.

The Sound of Seduction

PICK-UP LINE #109

"It was too expensive, but that tantric sex class was worth it."

"I agree," she said in her adorable accent. "Marriage means nothing, so zee groovy people should use it for our own lifes." She stared at me; I thought she looked a little sad. Hannah, Dave, and Sherrie were staring at me. Something was going on.

"What?" I asked.

They all looked at each other, and finally Hannah got up and sat in the chair Renata had vacated. She pulled it closer to me. She laid her hand on my thigh and flashed her big teeth at me. God, if they were supposed to be so open-minded, why did they all seem to want me to take the tall horsey one, when I obviously preferred the little graceful one?

"Lowell," Hannah purred. "Renata has a work visa, but I will have to go back to Sweden next month."

"That's too bad," I said, thinking, "So? You're blocking my view of Renata," and "Get your hand off my leg."

"Maybe not," Sherrie said mysteriously.

"Look, Lowell," Dave said in a take-charge voice. "Here's the deal. We think you ought to marry Hannah. Just for the green card. You live together for a couple months and then the immigration pigs lose interest in the case and everybody moves on. You've got straight-world cred because of the merchant marine, so you'd be perfect. What do you say?"

"Screw that" is what I thought. I stood up and moved away from the whole group. They all smiled at me expectantly.

"You don't take marriage seriously, do you?" Hannah said with a sneer. "Dave and Sherrie said you were this totally cool psychedelic painter."

"And that means I should *marry* you?' I thought. I was pissed; I'd been set up. They'd loosened me up with the incredible bud and sweet wine and sprung this on me. I didn't even like this girl.

But then I looked at Renata, and saw the hope shining from her pretty red eyes. She was obviously close with the "horse." I could help them stay together and maybe that would make Renata happy. Dave and Sherrie were my closest friends in this new city; they wouldn't steer me wrong, would they? I had a flash of paranoia that I was being uptight and uncool.

I stalled. "No, of course not. Marriage, ha! It's a patriarchal, uh, bad thing." I paused, then snorted derisively, "My *parents* are married."

Sherrie straightened her back and clapped her hands. "So you'll do it? Oh Lowell, that would be so groovy."

"My family is very wealthy," Hannah dropped her voice conspiratorially. "It will be worth your while."

"I'll think about it," I said. "I'll let you know." My buzz violently killed, I left and pushed my bike up the hill home.

I walked along the beach the entire next day, still puzzling it out. If I didn't believe in marriage, why not do it? The sky spread blue and cloudless above the endless sea. Maybe when a person was unsure, he should just do what would make the most people happy, for the karma. And undermining the immigration pigs *seemed* like working for the revolution.

But Hannah got on my nerves with her rich-girl entitlement and bossiness. I didn't want to talk to her, much less shack up with her. I eventually convinced myself that being pushed into something that felt so imprisoning was worse than a drag—it was a betrayal of the whole Age of Aquarius.

I went back to the warehouse the following day and told Sherrie no, I wouldn't do it. She argued with me and, when I wouldn't budge, stopped talking to me. Within a few weeks, though, equilibrium was back. The Swedish girls had moved on to L.A., and Sherrie stopped calling me bourgeois for *not* marrying an unpleasant stranger.

Visually Accurate

A photograph in dire need of a caption
Fran B., 27

THIS WAS A SETUP by my friend Lily. She said her friend George worked in the entertainment industry too, and we'd get along. He called me up and we had a nice chat. I had passes to an advance screening of a movie and invited him along. I thought we were ready to hang up when he said, "Hey, do you mind e-mailing me a pic? I'll send you one."

I did mind a little, but went ahead and sent a nice, and recent, shot of me. I laughed when his arrived: It was a picture of him in a bathroom, towel around his waist, shaving. He was very good-looking, but the exhibitionism was a bit of a turnoff in combination with the demand for a picture.

We got to the screening room a little early, and we'd just sat down when he picked up his phone, though I didn't hear it ring. I heard his half of a conversation indicating his office was calling him back in. "Oh come on, Joseph," he protested. "Can't this wait till tomorrow?" He hung up, turned to me sadly, and said it couldn't be avoided. I hadn't heard any voice coming from the phone, and I assumed I'd been very clumsily rejected. I stayed on but didn't enjoy the movie much.

> He hung up, turned to me sadly, and said it couldn't be avoided.

Two days later, he e-mailed me:

Fran, sorry to run out like that. I think you're going to make a great girlfriend for someone, but can I give you a piece of advice? Use a picture that looks more like you.

Hope there are no hard feelings, I'm just trying to tell the truth.

Peace, George

At first I deleted the e-mail and just raged to Lily and some other girlfriends about his behavior. But then I dug his note out of the Trash folder and wrote back. "I don't know where you got the idea you're such a prize, Mr. Towel Picture, but everything about you screams tiny penis. Glad I didn't have to find out in person."

No Cake

A scheduling disaster

Patty P., 40

THIS DATING DISASTER is entirely my fault. When I first got divorced, having not been on a date in more than fifteen years, I let a a coworker fix me up. The thought of romance with someone new was vaguely terrifying, but I felt it was time to move on. (Everybody certainly kept telling me so.)

Besides my nerves, another problem was that I really wanted to be somewhere else on the night we picked to meet. My ex-husband's brother and nephew's band was playing at the Bent Elbow, a local nightclub. I was torn. I really wanted to see them—it was important to me to keep up my friendships with my ex's family, as much as possible.

I also knew I shouldn't pass up a chance to try dating again, so I went on the date.

Ryan was very nice, good-looking, perfectly

acceptable. Just in case he turned out to be a dud, I had planned an emergency escape call. And somewhere between the first drink and the appetizers, my girlfriend Nancy rang my cell phone, right on cue.

"Oh, really? No, it's okay, I understand. Did you take his temperature? Okay. Don't worry. It's all right, I'll just come home, don't worry about it," Ryan heard me say.

"That was the babysitter," I told him sadly.

The date hadn't been going horribly, but I thought, why not have my cake and eat it too. A little date, a little Bent Elbow.

"I'm sure she's overreacting," I said, blaming the sitter, "but she says my son has a fever, so I'm going to have to cut this short."

I was halfway out the door as Ryan tried to tell me how much fun he'd had and that he would call me again soon. This was perfect: I could have my old-life cake now and eat new-life Ryan cake at a later date, when I was more hungry for it.

I sped out of the parking lot and made it to the Bent Elbow in twelve minutes, just in time to catch the end of the first set. I met my accomplice Nancy and we high-fived. I made my way to the small stage to say hi to the guys in the band. As I was hugging them all hello—thrilled by my deception—my nephew looked over my head and said "Hey, Ryan! You made it after all!"

"Ryan? That's a funny coincidence," I began, and then, right there at *my* bent elbow was Ryan, my date.

I thought he would either kill me or totally humiliate me. But he ignored me and went to shake hands with the bass player, my ex-husband's nephew.

"Glad you could make it!"

"Yeah, my date said she had to go home," he said, giving me a dirty look so subtle nobody else would see it.

As the band went backstage, I tried to recover. "Oh, you know these guys, too? I was just stopping by to tell them I couldn't make their gig because my son is sick . . . so I guess I better get going."

I turned tail and went home, having ruined my date *and* missed my night out with my friends.

Not surprisingly, I never got a phone call from Ryan.

Extra Booty

Off the stage and under the costume
Amanda C., 44

I'M AN ARTS JOURNALIST who was single for many years. Years during which, I admit, I wrote a disproportionate number of features about single, straight male artists.

Every May 1 in the city where I live, this performance artist I'll call Buzz organizes a wonderful group-participation piece in the park called "Mayday Pirate Mayday!" He distributes really easy sheet music that everyone can follow, costumes, and treasure hunt–type clues, and people end up singing and chanting and collaborating with strangers. In the event's third year, before it became an institution, I pitched a feature about Buzz and got the assignment.

I was online dating a lot at this time, and discovered that the photo of Buzz from his artist's website was also on Match.com. He had a charming profile, and he wasn't bad-looking. Once again, I was tossing the stone of an article at two birds: story subject and bachelor. (Dating is a lot like interviewing and vice versa.)

I first contacted him in the winter. He lived a few hours out of town, and we were both prolific e-mailers. Of the many things I love about my job, having carte blanche to ask questions may be my favorite. I found out he was four years divorced, no kids, somewhat lonely, and dying to spend more time at his apartment in the city. There was also some discussion of his art.

As the ground began to thaw, Buzz readied his props. And a strange and rare thing alighted in my life—a boyfriend! Dennis was also a fan of Pirate Mayday and was impressed that I was covering it for the Sunday paper. I managed to casually slip my new "taken" status into an e-mail to Buzz, and he absorbed the news with a networker's grace.

But I'd been hunting and gathering single men for too long to let a good one go to waste. I thought of a friend's friend, Mary, who did political guerilla theater. I put them in e-mail touch and soon got separate thank-yous from both Buzz and Mary.

Mary kept me abreast of their communications: He'd begged off meeting till after Pirate Mayday, understandably, and told her he'd be too busy to even e-mail until the event was over. But they were talking about going on a date after that, and she was excited.

On the day of the show, I said I'd like to meet him at his apartment to document the load-up of costumes and props. Buzz hemmed and hawed and said he was in the middle of renovations. Then he said he had to run, and then didn't call me back.

So I just went straight to the gathering place in the park to take notes on the event. Mary decided to come, too, to at least experience Pirate Mayday, and maybe to surprise him.

We got there early; no Buzz. A woman was handing out eye patches, sheet music, and stuffed parrots, and the two of us went up and asked if she knew where Buzz was.

MOTHER KNOWS BEST

LESSON #88

"Don't trust anyone with a tattoo or piercing. It's a sign of insecurity."

"No, can I help you?"

"Um. Maybe. Who are you?" I said.

"I'm Paula. I live with Buzz," she said, rummaging through a box of peg legs.

"Ah," I said, trying to process. "In the apartment here, the one with the renovations?" I asked stupidly.

"What renovations?"

Mary and I exchanged looks.

"Are you Buzz's roommate?" said Mary.

"No, his girlfriend. Who are you all?"

Mary guffawed quietly and stepped back. "I'm doing a story about him for the *Tribune,*" I said.

"Oh, here he is," said Paula, and six eyes shot suspicion. Buzz, a little older, shorter, and heavier than his picture, began a smile, then took in the sights: me, a little older, shorter, and heavier than my picture, and Mary, ditto. But we were clearly the two women—or two of the women—he'd begun e-romances with over the past few months.

He stopped and wheeled around. "Hey, Paula, can you keep handing stuff out? I forgot something!" He speed-walked away.

I glanced at Paula, I hope not pityingly, and bustled Mary away, calling out over my shoulder, "Thanks for your help." Then Mary and I sat on a bench.

"I'm sorry, Mary. I can't believe he's so duplicitous. He's on Match.com as single!"

Mary shook her head ruefully. "I know, you just assume the person who gives the city this gift is a good guy." She looked up with a smile. "I guess he'd like us to disappear, huh?"

"I'm doing a story, I can't."

"And I don't want to!" Mary laughed evilly. We went back to the costume box, now manned by neither Paula nor Buzz. Little wooden changing booths that looked like ships had been set up around the park. Mary went in one and came out in a sexy-wench bodice—the pirate look of choice for many well-endowed women, I noticed. She also wore an eye patch and a black skull-and-crossbones bandana around her head.

"I'm the avenging ghost of chicks on the side!" she cried, fluffing her cleavage.

I put a plastic hook-hand up my sleeve. "Aye, we'll make him pay for trying to plunder ye!"

And so we did. Six different sets of treasure-hunting instructions were distributed, so six streams of people ended up following a path of clues and performances through the park. We followed a map to the crook of a tree, where lyric sheets lay in a box. After we sang a song about a lonely pirate who never liked rum, a guy dressed as a skeleton led us to the band shell, where we took turns plastic-sword-fighting a British captain.

I knew from my research that Buzz wandered among the six groups all day. He showed up at the band shell mid-sword-fight, and Mary and I saw him before he saw us. We conferred behind a grove of big guys, then I stepped forward with my notebook.

"Buzz, this is a great happening. I can't wait to write it up. I'm a little curious, though, how Paula never came up in any of our interviews."

"Well, it's been on and off—and hardly relevant to the piece. She helps out, but so do a lot of people. Look, I gotta get to the next group."

Just then Mary leaped out in front of him with a small parrot stuffed between her breasts. She waved her plastic sword in front of his throat.

"And what about me, matey? What were ya gointa do with this booty?" She waved her ass lasciviously.

A few people turned away from the sword fight to this new drama.

"Heh, heh, you must be Mary. Heard good things about your work. Good to meet you."

"Ye've heard about me work, have ye?" she yelled. Heads turned. She bared her teeth and pointed her sword at them. "So was it some other Buzz who e-mailed me that me mouth looks kissable? And that he lived all by his lonesome?"

Now fifteen or so people had formed a circle around us.

"Yes, you do improv . . . " Buzz looked around at his fans and wiped his forehead with his bandana. "Big, big fan of your work."

"Again with me work!" Mary yelled, somehow getting even louder and more piratey. "And that's what ye do on Match.com, check out wenches' WORK?!"

"And what about me, matey? What were ya gointa do with this booty?"

The crowd looked at Buzz to see how he was playing this scene. A woman said to her neighbor, "Match dot com as in the dating site? I don't get it." She looked down at her instruction sheet for a clue. Others joined the murmuring as they studied their directions: "Do you see anything about Match?" "I think that's the guy who runs the whole thing." "Are we supposed to be doing anything in this scene?"

Buzz, locally famous for his improv chops, just stood there panicked, looking at everyone but Mary. Finally he pointed his plastic sword at the band shell stage, where the captain and his foe had just stopped fighting and were looking at him, too.

"Back to yer fight, mateys!" Buzz shouted weakly at them. "Happy Mayday everyone!" he called out, then turned and sprinted away, his plastic sword bouncing against his hips. "Mayday, mayday," Mary yelled after him, collapsing in laughter.

Buzz did not return to check in on our group. Mary ended up making out with a Blackbeard. For Paula's sake, I left the Buzz-Mary drama out of my newspaper story, but my editor still loved it.

I, Hannibal Lecter

With every bite, he sealed his fate
Mike T., 40

I **HADN'T BEEN DIVORCED LONG,** and I was set up with this woman by a coworker. I knew only a few things about her before we went out: She'd never been married but had a son my daughter's age; she was a vegan; and she liked to cross-country ski.

On our date, we went skiing. It was exhilarating, more fun than I'd had in a few years. She was beautiful and easy to talk to. I wanted to prolong being with her. We drove to a restaurant, where I had a burger and she had a salad, no cheese. Conversation flowed easily. When she ordered a second beer, I figured I had passed muster.

I walked her to her car and asked if I could see her again. She looked at me earnestly and said, "I'm sorry, Mike. You seem like a nice guy, but when you were eating that hamburger, I felt as if it was my own flesh you were eating."

I flinched. She kept smiling, and I waved weakly and left.

The next day I told my buddy Nigel the story, and he called her a "stupid cow." His tired Britishism was finally a decent punch line, so I laughed but I didn't mean it. I'd liked her a lot. And she was right: Eating meat is horrible if you think about it. I suddenly felt sorry for all the unsuspecting women to whom I'd be offering my disgusting divorced self.

MOTHER KNOWS BEST

LESSON #21

"Never trust a picky eater; nothing will please her."

Who's the Freak Now?

A little change in tone

Maggie M., 38

YOU CAN FIND A LOT OF THINGS on craigslist; Maggie thought she was lucky to have located a bona fide professor. His ad sounded fairly normal, and they went on a couple of okay dates.

Now, Maggie would be the first to admit that she has an amazingly low voice. So much so that she does sound masculine, though it's never been a source of confusion—before. According to the professor, she was putting out some mixed signals, which he addressed with the following e-mail: "I'm sorry, but before this goes any further, I have to know, are you a biological female? Don't be offended, you're very pretty and feminine, it's just that there are a lot of weird people on craigslist."

Maggie felt all the goodwill drain from her body. Dammit, he wasn't even that impressive and she'd been cutting him slack, talking herself into a crush, into giving him more of a chance, seeing his good qualities. But if he honestly thought she was a man, she certainly wasn't going to continue psyching herself up for him!

She got over her hurt feelings eventually, but she did register satisfaction when, a few months later, she saw that his ad had been changed to read: "Generous professor looking for Asian woman, monthly stipend available." Weird people on craigslist, indeed.

BLIND DATE OFFENSE #41
Challenging your date on his or her alleged gender

The Competition

A bilingual experiment

Sofia K., 35

I AM GREEK AND GOT MY PH.D. in psychology in an English-language program in Athens. The final step of my program was a clinical residency during which I would finally get to shrink the heads of actual patients. There were many locations to choose from. I had never thought of leaving my country, but for a one-year residency, New York City sounded exciting.

During my residency, I made a friend, Letitia. We talked first about our work and studies and then about men, very psychologically of course. Letitia had met her boyfriend through online dating and told me it was a very great, very mature way to meet serious men. She said it was better than bars. Americans all seem to say this about online dating, "better than bars." I told her I was not so serious—only one year here and then back to my country. She told me that there were also men online who liked fun and sex perhaps more than serious.

I posted my profile and many men wrote to me about their irritation with American women. Two men stood out of the herd, ones that didn't seem to want to meet me just because I was foreign. The younger one, Kurt, was funny and passionate, and his picture was beautiful. The older one, Michael, was literary and sincere. He was a playwright and he wrote that writers and psychologists were alike in being experts on the workings of the mind.

I wrote to both men for several weeks. The e-mails quickly became like love letters. I have never cheated and it felt strange to write to both as if they were the only one, but Letitia reminded me that they were probably writing to many women, that that is the way of Internet dating.

Michael was more persistent about meeting, and on our first date he took me to a very good Indian restaurant. He spoke very beautifully about many things and had much energy for a man his age (fourteen years older than me). He brought up the novel *The Last Temptation of Christ,* which I had also loved, and we talked about renunciation until it got very late.

Our conversation stayed in my head until our next date, three nights later. Again we talked and talked until we couldn't believe what time it was. This time we kissed good-night at the subway, which was more erotic than I expected and also very sweet.

For our third date, Michael asked me to join him at the reunion of an artist's colony he'd been to five months earlier, out in the country. He had made strong friendships in a short time. The colony was far away, but the reunion was in a Greenwich Village bar.

When I told Letitia of this plan, as I told her everything, she said, "Whoa, he's already introducing you to his friends?" Until she exclaimed, I did not find that odd. It seemed natural to want to know more about each other's lives.

Meanwhile, Kurt was pressing for us to meet. I told him that I would, but that I was too busy now—perhaps next week or the week after. He asked "Busy doing what?" and I said, "You know, work and things."

I dressed carefully for the reunion of the artists— not too sexy, not too conservative, not trying too hard, not too visible, not too invisible. Michael and I had held hands at the end of our second date, walking down the street before the kiss, but I didn't know what our protocol was now. I made my hand available to him as we walked into the bar, but he did not take it. Michael scanned the dark room and then waved and walked a little ahead of me to a big round table.

And there sitting at the table was Kurt. We recognized each other instantly from our profile pictures. He narrowed his eyes and mouthed, "Busy?"

I smiled nervously and looked at Michael. He was kissing cheeks and shaking hands and didn't notice my silent exchange with Kurt.

"So everybody, I want you to meet Sofia," Michael said in a voice too loud. "She and I met at MoMA, at the Richard Serra show."

I did not know what to do with my eyes. To look at Michael with my confusion would betray him in front of his friends. He was ashamed of Internet dating, not of me, I reasoned. He had brought me here on our third date to meet his friends, after all. We had both gone to that Serra show, but separately, before we met. I just wished I'd been prepared for the lie.

> He didn't notice my silent exchange with Kurt.

I did not want to look the way I felt, so I bared my teeth and pulled back my face. I hoped this looked like a smile. I passed my eyes around the table, nodding hello. Michael said, still loud, "Sofia, this is Lucy, Raoul, Marta, Matt, and Jeannie and, I'm sorry, I don't know you."

"Kurt," said Kurt, sticking his hand out at Michael and me. "Michael," said Michael.

Kurt turned to me. "Sofia, nice to meet you, or should I say, nice to see you? You look so familiar. I wonder if I also saw you at the Serra show?" He smiled. He was even more handsome than his picture, longer hair and beautiful eyes. He was taller than Michael and much younger.

"No," I said coldly. "I don't know you."

"Kurt's our friend," said the woman next to him, Jeannie. "He's thinking about going to the colony next year. He's a painter." Of course I knew that.

I saw with a sinking heart that the only two seats available were right across from Kurt. Michael pulled one back for me and sat to my left. I turned my chair almost perpendicular to Michael's, so I was staring at his profile and beyond, to the people to his left. The bar was loud enough so that I could hear Kurt's voice, but not his words. I avoided looking at him all night.

I was afraid I would be called upon to make conversation, but I had never seen Michael in a group. He was a true raconteur, telling stories that made everyone laugh. He would turn to me and ask how I was doing from time to time, and he kept his arm on the back of my chair. But he did not observe me closely enough to see my discomfort, because he was performing for the table. I stole one look at Kurt during one of Michael's stories and saw him staring at Michael, his beautiful lips twisted in disdain.

Michael was talking way more than anyone else. His shirt had come untucked, and I could see his belly, very white, pushing out a bit over his belt. Kurt looked like a young Elvis Presley.

Finally we left, and Michael hugged me close on the street. "That was really fun!" he exclaimed. "Everyone really liked you. Naturally." I'd meant to be irritated, but his exuberance atop the vulnerability of the lie made me warm to him.

"MoMA, huh?" I smiled.

He looked guilty. "I'm sorry, Sofia. I should have talked about it with you first, but I honestly didn't realize how embarrassed I was until I was standing in front of all those artists. I just didn't want to admit I was doing this bourgeois thing that gets advertised to desperate suburbanites."

I thought about making my own confession, that I'd met Kurt online. I opened my mouth, then shut it. Michael took my hand and we walked to the subway.

I was wearing beautiful underwear. Letitia had told me that the third date is often the sex date in America. That seemed fast to me, but I felt like I had known Michael for longer, and I was touched that he was introducing me to his friends. After our good-night kiss of the second date, I was looking forward to making love with him.

We stopped at the top of the subway stairs and faced each other. "Would you like to come back to my apartment for some absinthe?" he asked, touching my hair tenderly.

"No, not tonight," I heard myself saying, and we parted. I didn't read my book on the ride home, just let the evening swirl around my head like clothes in the washing machine. Michael was insecure and he lied; Kurt was beautiful. The night had confused me.

The next morning, I opened my e-mail. There was a love poem by Neruda from Michael. There was also a message from Kurt, subject line "I'm not ashamed of how we met." He went on to ask when he could take me out for a drink.

When Letitia asked me about my date, I just said that Michael's friends seemed nice and that he was very confident and charming in a group. In my own strange lie, when she asked about the end of the date, I told her I had my period and so went home alone. She would have pressed me for why I didn't have the sex date.

I agreed to see Kurt, without knowing what was my plan. When we had gotten our drinks and talked small for a while, I said to him, "Kurt, I must be honest. I have a keen affection for someone else that grew since you and I began to correspond."

"Who?" Kurt asked.

"Michael, you met him the other night."

"Him? How old is that guy anyway? Looking at the two of you, I just figured you were doing someone a favor or something."

But it was Kurt who did me the favor, as I rose to the defense of "the old guy." Five months after that conversation, Michael and I were married.

COMMUNICATION

Does life imitate art? Or do we just wish it did? A real-life "fail" date can certainly look an awful lot like Act One of a romantic comedy. And so we assume that an epidemic of miscommunication might just be the wacky prelude we'll one day laugh about—the prelude to the closing clinch, that slow-mo run into each other's arms.

The possibility of clouds magically clearing can be confusing for the romcom-hypnotized. We keep waiting for the plot twist, the mad dash to the airport that explains everything before the plane takes off.

Most blind daters, it goes without saying, never find the words that clear everything up. They're not in a vehicle for an adorable starlet—they're in a badly edited student film that they can only hope is a short.

You Want a Boy with Those Fries?

A leap behind the counter

Shantelle L., 17, with assists by Julia T., 16

JULIA: Me and Shantelle went out to McDonald's on a Saturday to have fun, hang out, and chill. So we ordered our McNuggets from this guy who looks like Michael Jackson circa 1991, got the Jheri curls and everything. And out of the blue, he says to Shantelle, "The guy in the back wants your number." I didn't have my glasses on, so I couldn't see who the hell the guy in the back was.

SHANTELLE: I could see two different guys in the back kinda looking in our direction, but I didn't know who they was eyeing. The one making burgers was sort of cute.

JULIA: I couldn't see them, but I knew who they were checkin' out. Shantelle had on a pink shirt, all tight and whatever, her hair all done. She was looking extra fly.

SHANTELLE: Don't I always look put-together?

JULIA: You looked extra put-together.

SHANTELLE: I was trying to look seventeen, because people always think I'm a little girl.

JULIA: Shantelle's mother never lets her go out. She's never talked to guys except her little brother. It ain't her fault she's so shy.

I am not shy. Anyone will tell you that. And I want to help Shantelle step up her game.

So after we got our food and sat down, I wrote her number on a napkin and I got back up to get some dipping sauce. I got in the same line. I didn't want to get Michael Jackson in trouble with his manager or whatever, so I slid the napkin across the counter and said kinda quiet, "You know that girl over there? This is her number. Give it to that boy in the back." And I kind of pointed my head at the guy I thought it was. Michael Jackson kept asking "You're not frontin' me? You're for real? You're not frontin'?" and I kept saying, "For real! It's her number!"

Shantelle had on a pink shirt, all tight and whatever, her hair all done. She was looking extra fly.

SHANTELLE: So the next morning I saw I got a text message at like two in the morning, and all it said was "Yo," and I wrote back, "Who this?" and he wrote "The dude from McDonald's," and I'm like, "Oh." And then my phone broke so we went back to McDonald's to tell him why I didn't write back.

JULIA: But Shantelle got all shy and scared, so I went over to Michael Jackson and I asked him who he gave Shantelle's number to. He pointed to this guy and said his name is Pedro. I looked back at Shantelle, like "That the dude you like?" and she shook her head.

SHANTELLE: I didn't know what to do!

JULIA: All I can say is thank god for me. I called burger guy over and said I meant for Michael Jackson to give her number to you.

SHANTELLE: I was so embarrassed! But he was nice. He came over and told me his name is James. He put my number in his phone and I put his in mine. (Sorry Pedro!)

JULIA: Sooooo Shan-telle, what happened on the date with James?

SHANTELLE: Now I'm embarrassed. We went to Bryant Park and we was just sitting there talking on a bench, and he said, "Why you so far away?" I was so nervous I was shaking and looking around, I didn't know what to do. He put his arm around me. It was cold outside, and he was in long sleeves and I was in short sleeves and he kind of put his shirt around me. It was nice.

The Sound of Seduction

PICK-UP LINE #42

"Hey, my friends bet me that I couldn't lift you."

I'd never been on a date before and I didn't want him to know that. I was already worried that he thought I was weird because I couldn't think of things to say. But he was funny. He told me all the boys at McDonald's were teasing Pedro that James had stolen me away.

JULIA: So, did you kiss?

SHANTELLE: I'm supposed to say that part? Did we kiss, Julia?

JULIA: Why you asking me?

SHANTELLE: I told you we did!

JULIA: Then we went into McDonald's, and he act like he didn't see her.

SHANTELLE: We were sitting right in front and I know he could see me, but he didn't wave or nothing.

JULIA: Then he texts her, "Why you looking for me at work?" like he was mad.

SHANTELLE: Well, I'm mad at him, too! Now whenever I go in there, all these boys look at me and start talking in Spanish. I know they're talking about me. It's embarrassing! I don't like going over there now.

JULIA: First of all, it was your McDonald's long before those boys got their jobs. How long you been living in that neighborhood?

SHANTELLE: Almost four years.

JULIA: Exactly!

SHANTELLE: It's not fair. I feel like going and telling him, "I didn't ask for your number, you was the one texting me." And the boys in there are like hound dogs, all looking at me when I'm just trying to go to McDonald's. That's his fault! What did I do? Why he can't just text me back?

JULIA: The hell with him. He's probably running game. Shantelle, he ain't worth it.

SHANTELLE (not believing her): I guess not.

BLIND DATE OFFENSE #77
Asking "When's the last time you had sex?"

Game Over

The trials and tribulations of RL (real life)
Star V., 34

I'M A GAMER. I love exploring and creating alternate universes. I'm active in the RPG (role-playing game) community; I love Second World and The Sims and games like that, all the way back to Myst and Dungeons and Dragons. I even make money creating fantasy environments for corporate parties.

Games aren't a distraction for me; they're more like a philosophy and a way of life. Making a game is not so different from trying to live ethically. I think of my life as a game where doing good things for other people gives you bonus points.

I especially love the optimism and sense of possibility among Internet geeks, and in that spirit I tried online dating. Sure, I'd heard the bad things, but I didn't want to close myself off to any fount of untapped potential.

Sadly, I soon found that people tended to be more dishonest with online dating than in either RL (real life) or the game environments online. When you are e-mailing someone, for instance, they have what I call Google brain, time to access information that might make them look smarter than they really are.

I had been talking to one fellow online for a couple of weeks. We were playing a bit of a game: He was trying to get me to guess what country he was from by giving me clues. The clues were a bit odd and chaotic, but I tried to be a good sport and played along. I thought I had guessed his home country correctly, and that's when I said, "Let's meet, and let's make it another game."

> When you are e-mailing someone, they have time to access information that might make them look smarter than they really are.

I created a treasure hunt that would eventually lead him to me. I e-mailed him a clue that would take him to a pay phone with a package hidden under it. The package contained a phone number and a quarter. The number was my best friend's. She would give him the next clue (plus she'd assess him for me).

My best friend's clue would lead him to a bookstore, to a book he and I both liked. Then to another book that had meaning for us, which would lead him to me, sitting with an atlas to show him where I believed he was from. I tried to keep this all light and playful. I set up most of my dates this way, so I know guys can get intimidated.

On the day of, I set everything up and went to the bookstore to wait. I was nervous—who wouldn't be nervous about meeting a new person and waiting for a game to work out properly? I waited and waited. I called my best friend to see if she'd gotten a call. No.

After three hours I called it quits and collected the clues and went home. In my inbox was a very angry message from him. He thought I was messing around. He hadn't even been able to follow the easy pay-phone clue and claimed that he saw me "run away" from the coffee shop by the phone booth.

But as it turned out, he'd sent a friend to the coffee shop to watch for me because he . . . well, he was a big weirdo who never intended to follow the clues in the hunt at all. (Or at least that's what he told me. I bet he just couldn't figure out the clues, but I will never know.)

Things quickly went downhill. I told him I wasn't interested in talking to him anymore, as I couldn't trust him. Everything dissolved into him sending me near-abusive e-mails and me doing my best to ignore him till he went away. He had been able to mask who he was on the Internet, but looking back I could see a few clues that might have revealed his true nature if I'd paid less attention to my game, and more to his.

The Moment of Truth

*Mayhem, blood, cops, and
enraged drivers are the sideshow*

Francesco G., then 21, and Eddie P., then 19

IT WAS THE LATE '70S, RIGHT, and maybe being gay was okay in San Francisco, but it wasn't okay in Asbury Park, New Jersey. Or that was what Eddie thought. So his version of himself was "I just haven't been with a woman yet, that's all."

The rest of the guys, we liked Eddie, and we were cool with it. We even told him, "You know what, Eddie? If you're a queer, that's all right. Don't worry about it."

But Eddie wasn't having that, and he was gonna make himself straight, dammit. So he said to me, "Francesco, come on, get me a date. Don't you know any girls who'll go out with me?"

I thought about it, and I says, "Well, I know a girl named Trudy, and basically, if you have a pulse, she'll sleep with you."

"She sounds perfect!" said Eddie, clapping his hands like a girl.

So my girlfriend and I and Eddie and Trudy drove into Manhattan and went to a bar in the Village. We had a couple drinks, we were all getting along, and Eddie suggested we go to *The Rocky Horror Picture Show* at midnight at the Waverly Theatre. I know, pretty obvious right? But Trudy don't get it, and she was all into it, and we went and Eddie told us all the things we were supposed to yell and we had a blast.

We went out to the car, it was 2 A.M., and now Eddie could no longer ignore the moment of truth. Me and my girl were in the backseat getting close. Eddie was driving and Trudy was kinda inchin' over toward him. I looked up and saw Eddie's face in the rearview; he was literally sweating. There was a goddamn traffic jam at the Holland Tunnel and Trudy figured the car was stopped long enough for her and Eddie to initiate contact. She popped in a piece of gum and scooted closer. Eddie fiddled with the radio and sweated some more.

Suddenly the car leapt forward, like Eddie floored it or something, and smashed into the car ahead. Trudy was thrown into the rearview mirror and her head was bleeding. The guy ahead of us was jumping out of his car, yelling "What the fuck," and charging back to Eddie's window. He saw Trudy's head, though, and just exchanged info with Eddie real fast, because we obviously had to get to a hospital.

Horns around us started blaring. Cops and an ambulance finally made it to us and cleared a lane for us to go back to St. Vincent's emergency room in Manhattan. The car was dragging some fender, but it drove okay.

And Eddie, I swear to Christ, was totally calm. The sweaty, nervous driver had been replaced by this, like, cool-headed doctor from *M*A*S*H*. He laid Trudy out on the front seat and bandaged her head with his T-shirt; he handled the cops beautifully. He took charge at the hospital, too, and stayed with Trudy till she got a couple stitches. At 5:00 A.M., my girl and I went to sleep in the car. At 6:30, Trudy was out of the hospital, she was fine, and we all drove back to Jersey.

Mayhem, blood, cops, enraged drivers, the emergency room—Eddie was obviously happier about all this than about kissing a girl. And do you know it *still* took him another ten years to come out, the poor bastard.

Landmine Landline

A dater overhears his own capsule review

Tom W., 32

IT WAS MY FIRST FACE-TO-FACE DATE with Ashley, an Upper East Side lawyer who'd gone to an Upper East Side private school. She was slumming on Nerve.com and by going on a date with me, a poet/drummer/office temp with four roommates. We had a nice conversation, though, and she told me about her conservative friend Mary who was scandalized that she was online dating. I could tell Ashley used Mary as her conscience or superego: "Mary says" covered all her doubts.

But Mary was no match for me—the date ended up in Ashley's girly bedroom, the teddy bear displaced onto the floor. The next morning we're lying there and the landline answering machine went off: "Hey Ash, it's Mary. How'd the date go with the hippie?" Ashley raced across the room. "Did he make you listen to his Grateful Dead tapes, *man*? Haaa-haa-haaaw—" Ashley knocked the answering machine off the table.

"Jack?"

"This drunk man could react badly"
Patrick N., 28

A FEW YEARS BACK, I joined my first Internet dating site. It took a few weeks to get my confidence up to chat with boys online, but I finally got there and was getting on nicely with a chap named Jack; we had loads in common and laughed at the same sort of things.

After a week or so of e-mailing, we decided to meet up the following week, after I visited some friends in Copenhagen. My Danish friends were having a fancy dress party with a biker theme; I wasn't hugely keen about the whole thing, but had decided I would try to find a funky biker-type jacket that could be reworn on some other occasion. And in talking up the Copenhagen weekend with Jack, I had promised I'd show him the jacket.

We agreed to meet at a pub we both liked right near his flat. It was very cozy, with good beer;

not a gay bar, just a neighborhood pub. I'm not that shy a fellow, but as I got ready to go on this, my first Internet date, my nervousness began to manifest as physical symptoms, which in itself unnerved me!

I got to the pub at a couple of minutes past our meeting time. A chap sitting at the bar looked up and shouted out "Nice jacket." I peered through the dim light—he looked something like the tiny photo on Jack's profile.

I went and joined "Possibly Jack" at the bar, ordered myself a drink, and offered him one. We started chatting nicely enough, and it soon became clear that he was drunk. He was quite loud and rowdy, but very personable. I knew I should just ask, "Are you Jack?" but the moment had passed. If he were Jack, it would be a stupid question; if he wasn't, then this drunk man, possibly heterosexual, could react badly.

I excused myself, and on my way to the loo wandered round the different rooms of the pub checking for a man sitting alone looking like he was waiting for someone. I didn't see one, and so I went back to my new friend at the bar, not knowing what to do. He was still being quite pally toward me. By then I'd become fairly sure he wasn't my date—it just wasn't feeling datelike, and on closer inspection, the

> As I got ready to go on my first Internet date, my nervousness began to manifest as physical symptoms.

resemblance seemed more tenuous. But if not he, then where *was* my date?

The agony abated somewhat when my drunken friend decided to go wandering round the pub (perhaps checking to see if *his* date had arrived?), leaving me alone at the bar. But by now a good twenty minutes had passed, meaning that my real date (if indeed he existed) was a good twenty-five minutes late . . . and who's twenty-five minutes late for a blind date around the corner?

Finally, forty minutes after the appointed time, Jack arrived, looking like his tiny photo and also, in the context of the other patrons, obviously gay. I walked up to greet him, so pleased that the drunken guy wasn't my date that I forgot to be pissed off at Jack's timekeeping. I got him a drink, and we found a quiet corner where we could chat, and where I could unburden myself of the trauma of the previous forty minutes.

Sadly, the evening didn't get any better. Jack wasn't terribly interested in what had happened. Or in my jacket, or in anything else about me. The only regret he seemed to have about his tardiness was that he missed out on an extra forty minutes to talk about himself. I found myself missing the drunk.

Reversal of Fortune

A game of telephone, complicated by the Internet
Jeff I., 29

AT FIRST, ONLINE DATING was totally bewildering. I'd have to replay conversations from face-to-face dates as I fell asleep, struggling to understand anything. I couldn't process "Oh, that was just polite interest!" or even "I don't like her that much." Not at first anyway. The first couple times, you really do assume that after all that e-mailing and I.M.ing, you'd be attracted to each other and hit it off perfectly. The dissonance is baffling.

But then everybody gets that and learns to navigate that stream of unspoken "I'm not attracted to you, Next!" It's cold, but it is the truth of the situation, and usually people can be human beings about it, not spring drama or ego on you.

Most sane people, at the end of a mediocre date, do the same thing. We shift back and forth at the top of the subway stairs. We look down, then up, we smile with our lips pressed together, we busy our hands. We telegraph mutual sympathy that we have to go on more of these dates. A few different girls gave me the perfect ending to such dates when they chirped, "Good luck!"

Angela was the first date, in fact, where I said "Good luck!" first. She was cool, nice, smart, cute, which made me feel not as guilty about not wanting her: Somebody would. And she seemed just as uninterested in me as I was in her. Our date was to a museum, and the line was long. We walked in Central Park a bit, then came back and saw that the line was much shorter. But she said, "I gotta go now."

"Okay, well, bye. And good luck."

"Good luck!" Angela lobbed back with equal ease. Nobody was pining. This online thing really could be done painlessly.

Coincidentally, the next two weeks of online dating happened to be rather brutal ego-and-hope-wise. Not one person on the dating site answered my initial contacts. Nobody wrote me except a Baptist lady in her fifties from Newark, which, nothing against, was just not my demographic. Except for her, I wasn't even getting viewed.

At the end of those two weeks, the phone rang and it was Angela. My first thought was disappointment that I hadn't read the situation right. I'd been proud of hearing those "Good lucks" so clearly. I thought I really had online dating figured out.

I was wrong, apparently. So did she think we needed a second date after all? Did I think that? What was my problem with her anyway? She was cute and smart and cool. I was almost thirty, nobody's idea of a material success, so what was I waiting for? What was wrong with me that I could so blithely assume Angela wasn't for me? Where did I get off being so picky?

LESSON #97

"It's as easy to love a left-handed guy as it is to love a Spaniard."
(Mom never made sense.)

"How's it going? How was your day? What are you up to?" Angela babbled.

"Fiiiine. Gooood. How was your day?"

"Well, I didn't get that client, the one in the brownstone."

I had no idea what she was talking about, but I have a crappy memory. I actually could not remember her profession. Something with clients. "That sucks. I'm sorry."

"So," she said tentatively, "I hadn't heard from you and I had a great time, so I figured I'd do the calling, not assume any gender roles, ha ha."

"That's nice. Thanks. Okay. So, do you want to get together again?"

"Yes." She sounded shockingly sincere, a sudden breach in the coolness. "Yes, I really do, Jeff. I do want that."

"Okay," I stalled for a second. God, I had learned nothing after all. I had misread this woman worse than any cyberdate in my eight-month history. She was seriously into me. "I remember Union Square was convenient for you, do you want to go somewhere around there again?"

Angela paused. "Wow. Okay, this is weird. I guess I just have to ask. You're Jeff the lawyer, right?"

"No, I'm Jeff the artist."

"Oh my god, I'm so sorry."

"No, it's fine, I was wondering why you'd called. I thought we didn't have much chemistry."

"Jeff the artist?" Another pause and then she laughed, too loud. "No way! Totally not attracted! Not even a little bit!" More hysterical laughter.

"Okay, okay, I got it. Good luck with the lawyer."

Schooled

Humanists need not apply
Edward H., 43

HER **"FIVE ITEMS I CAN'T LIVE WITHOUT"** were "dictionaries, free advice, inner monologue, coincidence, and memory." Her "Why you should get to know me" was "It's destiny"—still my favorite answer of that inane question.

Of course I look at the pictures. But glimmers of brilliance and complexity and book-love generally make up the scent I track like an e-bloodhound. And so I crafted my "casual" first e-mail in a mere four hours (that included Web research to check poetry quotes). Yeah, I was procrastinating.

There was a three-day written buildup to the date. Sexy play-scolding, name-dropping, and extravagant compliments of each other's prose. She told me she'd published a book of poems "about how nobody loves me" and that she was an adjunct professor teaching creative writing. She only gave me her first name. She managed to work her black bra and garter into an e-mail. I was very excited for this date.

At the bar, I liked her right off. I already liked her, really, so all I did was continue liking her. She was funny and sharp, a great talker. She wasn't physically beautiful, but her personality and intellect were captivating. I was smitten.

We were getting along well, and then she asked me where I went to college. "Actually I'm a high school dropout," I explained. "But that's a story for our second date."

For most of the date, her face had been arranged in a soft smile, relaxed. After my confession, her smile vanished and her brow furrowed.

She pressed me. I tried a few times to sidestep the questions without seeming defensive. But she was like a lawyer interrogating a witness, and so I told the story of how I came to drop out. I think it's a good story and one that makes me look like a free-thinker. I went my own way. But it was clear she simply hated that I was uneducated.

So this was the end, suddenly and irrevocably, of our beautiful relationship-in-potential.

I tried to indicate by my demeanor that I didn't mind her questions, but of course I did. It was weird, because the judgment was mutual—she judged me for dropping out, and I judged her for how she reacted to learning about it. So this was the end, suddenly and irrevocably, of our beautiful relationship-in-potential.

And while it was happening, I kept thinking things that added up to "Please don't do this to us." I'd barely finished my narrative when she put down some money and walked out of the restaurant alone.

I paid the bill and left. Walking slowly up the street, I went over the conversation in my mind to make sure the wall we hit was indeed my level of educational attainment.

Suddenly, I remembered the name of a poet we'd both been reaching for before the terrible revelation. I saw her back moving away from me down the street a block away. I had a sudden urge not to salvage, but to normalize, to offer some equivalent of "No hard feelings," a better vibe to part on. I ran down the street to shout "It's Cesar Vallejo!" and then, "I know it would have bothered me, so I figured I'd put your mind at rest. Good night."

I reached her and said, "Hey Olivia, I remembered! It's Cesar—"

She wheeled around, her eyes narrowed, mouth set. "Are you following me?" she asked.

"What?" I sputtered, "I just wanted to tell you I reme—". She pulled her cell phone out of her purse as if to call for help. I shook my head and backed away, then took off down the street. I felt like crying.

I couldn't let it go, and worked out some of my frustration where I usually do—on the Internet. By piecing together various bits of information she provided during the date, I was able to figure out her full name. This led to reading some of her poetry online. Happily, I didn't like any of it.

I also went back to her profile and noticed ruefully that the educational snob put *Get Your War On*—great, but a *comic book* for crissake—as her "Last Great Book Read." I also saw in a new light her clever response under "Religion": "Humanist (non-practicing)."

Falling

With a helping hand
Sadie P., 32

WE MET AT THE BAR. Two things were immediately apparent: 1) He was extremely tall. 2) For my taste, he was too self-consciously hipstery. But he seemed very nice, and so I thought, well, maybe I'll make a friend. Conversation wasn't earth-shattering, but it hummed along. I came back from the bathroom ready to order another beer. Mostly because beer is delicious. But before I reached my seat, he swiveled around and said, "So, I'm just going to be honest."

Honest?! After one beer? What kind of horrible joke was this?

He went on, tilting his head and smiling to express gentleness and sympathy: "I really don't think we're vibing, so I'm just going to call it a night."

I paused for a moment, a moment during which I hoped he felt extremely uncomfortable. First of all, who says "vibing"? Second of all, I was fully aware that this was not a good date. But I was raised among humans, and taught how to interact with other members of the species without damaging their psyches. Which is why I calmly faced him and said, "Hmm, so is this how you end all of your dates?"

At which point, his bar stool spontaneously catapulted backwards. I swear to god I didn't touch it. Because he was so tall, it seemed to be happening in slow motion. He had a long way to go before he reached the floor.

When he did, I helped him up.

Plenty of Akilter

Alice doesn't live here anymore
James M., 42

T**HEY SAY THERE ARE THIRTEEN** single women for every single man in Washington, D.C., yet I did not enter my current state of domestication until I was forty. The problem was that in the city of overachievers, of high school class presidents, I prefer women who are slightly akilter.

I got set up a lot. One time, a married friend of mine met this attractive, very talkative, high-energy woman on a business flight. Recognizing in her that strange gleam that always drew me in, he got her information and suggested I call her.

The first date was a long one, with plenty of akilter. In the second bar we went to, she told me she had her pilot's license and that she'd flown her plane under (under?) New York's George Washington Bridge. After the third bar, she led me into a Georgetown bookshop in whose bay window she began to dry hump me. This boded well. Then came a stumbling walk in the snow back to my car, with a stop for her to pee crouching between cars in a parking lot. I drove us back to her house; our night was fun but not completely unscary. The next morning, she asked me to drive her to retrieve her car.

On the way out, I asked her about the address labels on some letters she was mailing—her name was Boyd but these said Klein. She explained that Klein was her maiden name, Boyd her married one.

"Married name?" I asked, as casually as I could.

"Yeah," she rolled her eyes with the sort of mock exasperation befitting a mix-up at the coat check. "I married this guy Walter Boyd a few years ago in England, but things didn't work out and I moved back to D.C. I kind of forgot about him until tax time, and my accountant said I should divorce him. But when I called him, his phone was disconnected, and letters didn't reach him either. My lawyer ran ads in newspapers in England and D.C., and she's pretty sure that's sufficient as service of process when you can't find someone."

"Pretty sure?"

"Yeah. There might be some time left for him to respond, so I'm not sure if we're still married. I should find that out, huh?"

When I dropped her at her car, she asked me to follow her back to her house, and I said yes before finding out why. Once there, she asked me to assemble two Ikea bookshelves. It was such a strange first-date request that I couldn't figure out how to say no.

She watched me work, didn't so much as hand me a screw, and then upon seeing the shelves constructed, decided she didn't like them and asked me to help her return them to Ikea. "No, I really have to get home," I said, and she fumed. I left anyway. As I pulled out, she was dragging the shelves out to the street and strapping them—still assembled—to the top of her car.

There were more than enough red flags to never call her again, but I somehow ended up with a glove she insisted on getting back (I swear I think she planted it on me). When I returned her call to arrange a glove handoff, I reached one of her roommates, who told me they had thrown her out in the last two days and did not have a forwarding address.

Trust Me, We're Soul Mates

Stranger than he looked

Louise E., 41

I **SIGNED UP ON DHARMAMATCH,** the dating site for spiritually inclined people. I'd online dated enough to know there was no point to a long e-correspondence before a date—it just gives you the false impression that you know someone, ultimately making the blind date process just that much more complicated. So I didn't know anything about Frank except that he identified himself as a spiritual guy and seemed thoughtful, open, age-appropriate. And was looking for a long-term relationship.

We met at a Starbucks in the afternoon. He was late and when he walked in, I saw that he was better looking than his picture implied. I also saw that he was partially paralyzed, and had to sort of drag one of his legs behind him. My first thought was "That's a big thing not to tell someone." My second was, "I guess I understand; maybe a lot of people wouldn't meet him." His handicap tapped into my do-gooderness and so I resolved not to mind.

He told me it had happened in a car accident long ago and he'd been through years of rehab. We talked about that and then other things, our jobs. The conversation wasn't great, but nothing awful, just sort of blah. Then out of nowhere, he leaned across the little round Starbucks table and kissed me on the lips.

> His handicap tapped into my do-gooderness and so I resolved not to mind.

I jerked my head back and stammered, "Oh, that's not cool with me." This was not about his disability—I swear!—it's just that there had been absolutely no precedent for that kiss, no leading conversation, no dreamy gazing, no nothing. We were strictly in the "And how many siblings do *you* have" zone.

"Why, what's wrong?" he asked.

I didn't get to answer. He launched into a long monologue about how he could tell right off that we were soul mates. He could see in my eyes that I was going to be good for him. "You don't know it yet, but you're going to realize we were made for each other."

At this point, it was clear that this guy was more than a little off-center. I was alarmed, actually feeling sort of unsafe and wanting to escape, but afraid of making him angry. I tried to bring him down but keep him calm, not get him pissed off. "Well, I'm not sure how anyone would know that this soon, but I hear you," I said. Finally I told him I had to get going. He insisted on walking me to the subway.

My heart was in my throat. As we walked, he kept saying, "You're going to see how good we're going to be together," half-dragging his foot behind him. I wanted to race away but felt too guilty, imagining how often he'd been left behind in his life.

When we finally got to the station, he tried to kiss me again but I preempted with the cheek. I ran down the subway stairs. By the time I got home, indignation had conquered guilt.

"Not a Date," Insist Both Parties

A friendly offer among friends
Clark K., then 39, and Erica T., then 28

CLARK

I moved from D.C. to San Francisco for four months, short-term. I was staying with my friend Lance and his wife and kids. Lance had just found out that his second daughter was not actually his, and the marriage would be over within a few months. Meanwhile, my wife of eighteen years and I had separated four or five months previous.

Life, especially the love part, was grim, and I was anxious to get out of that house and meet anyone I could. I'd gotten Erica's number from a friend. I was thinking, just a contact, not a date.

ERICA

I had this schizophrenic sense of him. My friend told
me I'd met him, but from all her descriptions, I was
thinking of someone else, not nearly as cute. I was
twenty-eight and he was almost forty and divorced,
and those seemed like big obstacles to me.

My two friends had spoken so highly of him that
I was interested in him as a person, but I wasn't
thinking of it as a date.

I'd only been in San Francisco for five months.
I was excited to meet new people. I hoped for a friend
to go to art things with.

He called on a Friday night, which I thought was
funny, but we had a nice chat. I told him about this
Bill Viola show at the museum and he said "I went to
that yesterday." I was impressed that he'd been in town
only a week and had already been to an art show.

CLARK

She was on the other line with her mother, and I
thought that was cute. We were wondering how we'd
recognize each other. I said, "I have brown hair and
I will probably be wearing a brown jacket and brown
pants." As soon as I said that I realized how stupid
it sounded, but it was true. Like a female bird, I am
predominantly brown. She laughed.

Monday came and I walked by the theater and saw this person sitting on the pavement. She popped up and gave me a hug and said, "Welcome to San Francisco," which was really sweet.

ERICA

I'd ridden my bike to the subway and was sitting on the sidewalk drinking coffee and waiting for the plain guy, and then this cute guy walked up and said, "Erica?" I said, "Clark?" and I jumped up and hugged him.

I'd been pretty lonesome, I missed my life in D.C.

CLARK

We sat next to two gay guys who told us which crepes to order and helped make it not so focused on the two of us, more of a fun group thing. I wasn't thinking of it as romantic.

She suggested we go for a beer down the street, and then it started feeling more like a date, a good date. She ordered a second beer, and that was my cue that she was enjoying herself. We had to leave before midnight, though, because that's when the subway closes in San Fran.

ERICA

At dinner we found all our layers of D.C. people in common, events we'd both attended.

Then we went to this documentary about smoking. And after that, to a place nearby to have a beer. We were chitchatting away and I ordered a second beer. Then I looked at my watch and realized my midnight subway deadline was approaching.

He said he'd drive me home. I thought, "Hmm, this is a date." Still, I wasn't having boyfriend fantasies; I knew that he'd just separated from his wife, and that he was only in town for four months.

CLARK

I didn't have anything else to do, so I said "I'll drive you to Oakland; I've never been to Oakland."

We went back to her cool little tree-house apartment and she pulled out a joint and we talked on the couch till 4:00 in the morning.

ERICA

Then I realized there was a guy in my apartment at 1:00 in the morning, and that made me nervous, so I asked him if he wanted to smoke pot, which either makes me paranoid or relaxed. But with him I was relaxed and the conversation was great.

We were sitting on the couch and I distinctly remembered my friend telling me he was a music geek, so I put on Belle and Sebastian to be cool. Then I put on Leonard Cohen thinking, "He's older, he'll like Leonard Cohen." I asked if he wanted to put on an album, and he put on Cowboy Junkies.

CLARK

She put on Belle and Sebastian when we first got there. I'd never heard them, and we talked about music. Then she put on Leonard Cohen and then I put on Cowboy Junkies, which she said later she read as a cue that it was romance time.

So it's 4:00 in the morning, we're both pretty tired and it's time to go to sleep or something. I could have gotten back in the car, but instead I took off my shoes. She said "Would you like some pajamas?" and I said, "I usually don't wear pajamas." I swear I said it innocently; it's true, I don't.

Not so innocently, I offered to give her a backrub and she said, "Yes, let's go to the bed."

ERICA

He said, "I gotta get going" and took off his shoes. I said, "Are you going home barefoot?" and he said, "Oh, I guess I'm giving mixed signals."

When I said "You can spend the night," I still wasn't thinking of it being sexual; it seemed like a friendly offer to me. He asked if he could give me a back massage and we totally had sex.

CLARK

It was nice to wake up there.

I drove back to the city in a daze, thinking, "I didn't expect all that to happen." I called her later that day and invited her to a rough-cut of a documentary

I was working on (i.e., a date with all the people I knew in San Francisco).

ERICA

In the morning, while I was in the shower, he went through my fridge and made coffee. I liked that he was making himself helpful, that I didn't have to play hostess. And we stumbled through our workdays and he called me that night. We've been together ever since, and now we have a son.

BEHIND THE
FOURTH
WALL

These stories have to come from somewhere. I cast my web World Wide, but some I found closer to home. (Full disclosure: I introduced "Clark" and "Erica"—and they very graciously keep thanking me, even when I don't remind them.)

The following three stories are the closest of all—I'm not using "we" as an affectation here. I'm out there trying my luck with strangers and reaping the strange, sad stories too. Every Acme product has backfired in my face, but I remain convinced—for no defensible reason—that next time it's going to end differently.

Settling

His story ended ours

Virginia V., 47, and Pepe L.P., 35

IT BEGAN ON A DATING SITE called OKCupid, where I've maintained one of several profiles for an embarrassingly long time. Into my OKCupid profile, I added that I was looking for dark tales of blind dates for a book. I also posted a call for stories in an OKCupid discussion board about dating.

Several days later, I checked my trap. I'd gotten nothing but the very young discussing their favorite two questions: "How many sex partners is too many?" and "Is making out cheating?" There weren't even any too-small stories for me to throw back in the cyberpond. Just as I was about to log out, a redhead with a Spanish handle I.M.ed me and said he had a good story.

I clicked into his profile and found that he was a French subprime mortgage specialist, twelve years younger than me, who had recently lost his job. He typed into I.M., "I was living in Paris and she in Zagreb; we met in Vienna and stayed together for years."

I typed back, "Sounds good. This is a stupid way to tell it, call me" and typed my number. The phone rang seconds later. "Okay, so, how had you initially made contact if you were in Paris and she was in Zagreb?"

He paused, said in a cute accent, "What do I get if I tell you this story?"

I thought, does he want money? "What do you want?"

He said, *un peu* like Pepe Le Pew, "To take you out."

I looked back at his profile. Under "The Most Private Thing I'm Willing To Admit Here" he'd put his credit card number and expiration date. It was a hilarious use of that slot. And I was attracted to his picture.

"All right, but I'm bringing my notebook."

Pepe (not his real name) made a Wednesday date for a wine bar between our two neighborhoods. He subsequently pushed our date back to Friday as he'd lined up a job interview for Thursday morning and he wanted to be fresh.

I was pleasantly relaxed about the reschedule because I didn't care. I could never love a Wall Street Master of the Universe. And if I were to take a walk on the dark side and date a finance guy—for the experience, to be open-minded—he should at least be rich. Call me classist, but a broke subprime mortgage expert is at the far end of lose-lose.

I found out that week that D. W. Griffith's *Intolerance* was showing at the cineaste temple Anthology Film Archives, on Friday night only. I'd wanted to see it on a big screen for years and was ready to go it alone—it's hard to scare up a date for a three-hour silent movie from 1916.

But why not try? Ready to be refused, I called Pepe and floated the idea. I told him the particulars and waited for a torture joke. "Sure," said Pepe. "I'll meet you there."

LESSON #19

"InterestED is interestING."

He was cuter than I thought he'd be. And he was more than a good sport about the movie, which was shown with no accompaniment whatsoever. It was truly silent, so we heard every burp and sigh there was to hear, plus several gurgles from my stomach.

I was in fact the philistine who whispered, early in the third hour, "Want to leave?" He was ready to stay, but agreeable. The circulation returned to our haunches as we strode to a cluster of bars, laughing about the earnest intertitles and crude beheadings. He also filled in my patchy knowledge of the Huguenots, featured in the film. I liked him more than I'd expected.

We found a not-too-loud-or-crowded lounge and settled on a couch. He bought us wine and sat down. We clinked, and he began his story.

• • •

On a European dating site, Natalia claimed to live in France, which she loved. It turned out she only *wanted* to live there. Our e-mails and calls were very flirtatious and hot. About a week in she confessed that she actually lived in Croatia. This was a few years after the war ended, and it was not good to live there, especially if you were a Serb, as she was.

She admitted her geography lie, then typed that she had a week planned in Vienna with her mother. Perhaps we could meet there?

Her mother would be occupied with the friend she was staying with. I was never clear on whether Natalia was invited to the friend's or not; I booked a hotel room and we stayed there together the whole week. I met her mother twice and we liked each other.

We came out of that hotel a long-distance couple. For every three or four times she came to Paris, I went to Zagreb and stayed with her and her mother. Natalia was a chemist, but wanted to become a businesswoman in a European capital. I was liaising between Internet start-ups and venture capitalists in those cities, so we traveled together a lot, too, eating brilliant food, making love, plotting our rise. London was our favorite city.

I loved being with her, but I realized after eight or ten months that I wasn't in love. I was not in awe of Natalia. She cared for me more than I for her, and that made me uncomfortable. Our one-year anniversary went uncelebrated. The day after that, she said, "You want to be released, don't you?"

I told her I loved her and wanted always to be friends, but yes, we should end the romance part of our relationship. My feelings were not strong enough.

She took it well; within a month we were back to e-mailing our same sort of e-mails minus the flirting and sex talk. We went from signing a whole row of Xoxoxooxxooxoxoxoxo's to just x or, when we exchanged confessions, xo.

I've always admired Natalia's power to make things happen. She got her employer to let her take over some marketing for the firm, and she came to Paris often. One night, we went dancing with a big group of my friends and had a great time. My friends all liked her, and she was spectacular in the club. I felt the old feeling. We ended up in bed.

We understood each other so well. She knew it didn't mean we were back together and never bothered me like that. We went back to the old way. We'd share intimate details of our lives on the phone because neither of us had found anyone else to tell. She told her mother everything, but still needed me for the young and cosmopolitan male viewpoint.

I gave her dating advice much more than she did me. She was my best friend.

She found out on her twenty-eighth birthday that she'd gotten a great marketing job in London. I was very jealous and also excited to visit her there. Just then, the Internet bubble broke and I lost my job.

I took a longer trip to London than planned, on a much lower budget. It was strange to have finite money in such an expensive city. Natalia was very comforting and generous, but I wouldn't let her pay my way. She was reeling from the costs of London, too. Her flat was expensive and small.

We had great adventures during my two weeks there, and I slept on the couch till the very last night, when we fell into her bed after a party.

We understood each other so well. We went back to the old way.

My apartment seemed dingy and lonely when I got back. I went straight online and began looking for jobs in London. Interviewing meant a few more visits. Natalia and I agreed over e-mail that we'd made a mistake the last night. I stayed on the couch through all these visits.

I got the job; it paid much more than I'd ever made. As soon as I told her, Natalia invited me to move in and split the rent with her.

"Where would I sleep?"

"In my bed. It's big. I think we could stick to our agreement."

Perhaps you think I am crazy that I said "Good idea" and packed. To us it seemed normal.

The chaste arrangement lasted less than a week. Both of us were back in the money, and living well felt like love. She still didn't move my heart the way I wanted, but she was more fun in the clubs than any woman I'd known, an ideal cross between girlfriend and friend. The people we knew in London called us the perfect couple, even after I told them that there wasn't enough fire.

A year after I moved in, Natalia decided to go to business school in America. She made it sound so smart that I joined her in the search for B-schools. She got accepted; I didn't. Off she went to Phoenix, Arizona.

I couldn't afford the flat by myself and lived with a horrible roommate I found in the newspaper for three or four months. Then I went back to Paris. It took me a while to find even a mediocre job. I lived with my parents in the apartment where I grew up for a brief and embarrassing time.

The next year, I got the call, from New York University. Two years later, I took my M.B.A. to a bank where they taught me to bundle mortgages. I whipped up money like meringue.

We visited two or three times a year. Her Phoenix friends, mostly the young wives of her B-school comrades, looked at me warily. Our relationship has always been hard to explain.

A year ago, Natalia's mother died. Natalia flew
to Zagreb just in time to say good-bye. She stopped
over in New York on her way home from the funeral.
She requested a wine bar near my apartment, and
I prepared to be the good listener for the evening.
She adored her mother; they always came running to
each other first for understanding and other feminine
comforts.

Natalia talked about her mother some. I tried to
hold her hand, more in friendship than anything, and
she jerked it away, suddenly angry. "Dammit, I'm about
to turn thirty-five. I've met every bachelor within fifty
miles of Phoenix who's on Match.com." She cradled
the hand with her other one, protecting it. "I haven't
met anyone I like as much as you, but I have to keep
my distance. I'm not your dream, and I deserve to be a
man's dream. I'm not sleeping with you anymore."

"Okay, that's fine. We won't. But I'm someone who
loves you and who knew your wonderful mother. So
give me your hand."

She looked down. "Maybe I won't be a man's dream,
who knows? More than a man, now, anyway, I want
a child. I went online to find out about adoption. I'd
rather adopt a child and know it's only mine from the
start. The worst thing would be to marry a guy, have
his baby, and then he leaves us."

"That's absurd," I answered. "Even a father who
leaves has given you some help at the hardest time and

has some interest in his kid's well-being. And the baby is part of you. Don't you care about any of that?"

"Not as much. I just want a baby before I'm suddenly forty."

Back at my apartment, she asked if we could sleep in the same bed in T-shirts and underwear, no fooling around. I said of course, and she cried in my arms. We hugged a long time at the airport, and called and e-mailed more often for a while.

I visited her a few times and respected her request for no sex.

Just this year, Natalia got a job in Santa Barbara, California. She rents a big house there. She still talks to me about adopting and also about online dating to find a man who's her dream and she his. But her new job and her house have become her focus.

Two months ago, most people in my division lost their jobs, including me. Natalia has asked me to come live rent-free in her house.

I'm thinking about going.

She wants that baby. We really know each other; maybe that's more important than feeling awe.

It's not for escape. I've been in New York four years, and I love it. The city's full of beautiful, smart women to date, and so much to do. I'm not scared about work. We can't stay down in this trough for too long. The country needs banks so banks will be okay. I'll just have to learn some new recipes.

But I get lonely. I want to be with someone every day. And I want a child, too.

• • •

The two of us looked into our wineglasses for a moment. Then Pepe turned to me and asked, "How about you?"

"What about me?"

"Do you want to have children?"

"I'm forty-seven years old."

"So?"

"So that means that's not happening."

"Oh." He looked down at the floor and then at me and smiled sadly. "Then we are doomed."

I thought to myself, "Pepe, not your real name, if we weren't doomed by your career, you certainly doomed us by telling me that story!" I didn't even primarily mean his unavailability, since I hadn't been interested anyway. It was more what the story revealed about his character. I thought his plan to go impregnate Natalia after dumping her repeatedly—especially when the one thing she didn't want was to be left by the baby's father—was itself doomed. And selfish and wrong.

People to whom I told the story said I was being too hard on him—that he was just a guy I met mid-settle, making his peace with marrying a friend and not a dream. And, they pointed out, Natalia's a grown-up.

Nobody's making her offer to take in Pepe every time his opportunistic ass gets fired.

But still, it seemed sleazy to take advantage of her generosity. I suspected Pepe, a man who gambled away other people's money for a living, of liking the challenge. Could he seduce his friend into giving up her dream of being adored by a husband who'd stick around to raise their kid? I think he got interested when she told him to back off.

What I said was, "I wondered why you wanted to go out with someone so much older than you anyway."

He smiled and gave a tiny Gallic shrug. "Because in the meantime, a man wants to be with a woman."

I laughed in disbelief. "I see, a little cougar action before you go start your California family?" I made claw hands and hissed.

He missed the sarcasm, just nodded enthusiastically and asked if I wanted another glass of wine. I declined.

"You Wish"

A relentless avalanche of badness
Virginia V., then 46

THIS IS ANOTHER OKCUPID GUY, one I met about a year before Pepe. He was tall, handsome, a couple years younger than me, and a D.J. with long hair. He seemed cool and was witty on e-mail. I was flattered that he initiated contact.

We lived close enough to each other that we arranged to meet at a bar between our neighborhoods, one we could both walk to. My step had an optimistic bounce as I made my way through a beautiful fall night.

The bounce was crushed by an avalanche of badness so relentless that I never even had time to feel disappointed. I watched safely from an ever-higher perch of incredulity, a protective response to the emotional danger I sensed.

First he's half an hour late, for which he does not apologize. Then his voice is so soft that I—and the bartender—keep irritably barking, "What?" and still he won't turn up the volume. It's got to be passive-aggressive; it certainly doesn't seem a flirtatious way to draw me—or the bartender—closer in.

I figure out how to decipher his frequency just as he starts bragging about the antique record he bought earlier that day for $20,000. What do you say to that? "My, you certainly are rich"? I ask who made the record.

"An obscure '60s garage rock group."

"Really? I love that kind of music, maybe I've heard of them."

First he's half an hour late, for which he does not apologize.

He snorts derisively. "You haven't, trust me."

All righty then. He lists band names that I indeed don't know for ten minutes or so, tracing their journeys through record labels I've never heard of. I slump. He tells me, "I thought your profile said you were tall. Or is it just your posture making you seem short?"

I sit up straight and defend five feet eight inches as sort of tall. But he goes off on a bizarre lecture about body types. He says how awful it must be to be short, but fat people are the worst—and it's their fault. His little rant culminates in "Fat people have no empathy." I think longingly of several large, empathic friends I'd so much rather be with now, telling the story he is turning himself into.

He keeps the offense coming. Of a wildly unpopular stadium-and-skyscraper complex to be built right near my home, he says, "I hope they build Atlantic Yards; that neighborhood is a slum."

Then he asks me what famous person I get told I look like—a dumb game. I say, "You go first," and he says, "Neil Young." I half-heartedly say, "No, you look way better than him" (he did), hoping to end the game. But he insists, so I say, "Well, a handful of people have told me in the last few years that I resemble the mom on the TV show *The Gilmore Girls.*"

He snorts, "You wish!"

I wish I could say I thought of the perfect retort, but a stunned silence was all I could muster. Released from any pressure to politely end the evening, I pled fatigue and hightailed it out of there.

BLIND DATE OFFENSE #4
Gratuitous commentary on blind date's physical appearance

....

Why Not?

....

Possibility saves a life
Andy P., 41

ANDY ALWAYS CARRIES A SAXOPHONE, just in case
someone needs music. A short, sturdy Brit with
a big jaw hoisting a big smile, he makes new friends
everywhere he travels and crashes with *their* friends
on other continents. His permanent residence is a
boat on the Thames.

I have a small cameo in Andy's blind date story,
which doesn't end in a romantic match. And that's
the point. Let Andy be a lesson to weary daters
everywhere: Too narrow a focus on that theoretical
spouse keeps you from adventure, serendipity,
friendship—in short, from all the possibilities that
come out of *not* seeing the person in front of you in a
utilitarian light.

I met him at a pumpkin-carving party, through
friends. A year before that, he'd gotten divorced from

his high school sweetheart, sold his house, and started traveling the world. He was in New York for three weeks, then off to Vancouver. We hit it off, and when a friend invited me to march in the West Village Halloween parade with his advocacy group, I invited Andy. He was, naturally, game.

Our group, Killer Coke, marched up a gauntlet of cheering revelers leaning over the blue police barriers. We repeatedly acted out the murder by narcoterrorists of union organizers in a Coca-Cola bottling plant in Colombia, a situation Andy and I got educated on as we marched. I played one of the thugs likely hired by Coke, and had an alarming amount of fun screaming at the union leaders and shooting them with a plastic gun. Andy improvised a jazzy march on his sax, veering into military music and dissonant honks for the murders, a soundtrack the activists loved. He and I both stopped drinking Coke for good after that night.

Too narrow a focus on that theoretical spouse keeps you from all the possibilities that come out of *not* seeing the person in front of you in a utilitarian light.

We hung out a few more times before he headed west. But no romance—we'd wordlessly become platonic pals. One night as we walked down East Ninth Street, Andy told me he'd been checking out the online personals. We looked at the bodies filling the sidewalk around us and agreed that the people of such a dense, not-shy metropolis shouldn't *have* to online date. It made no sense. Yet everyone I knew in New York was on Nerve.com. I told him he should check it out.

He dove right in, treating the profiles as a crash course in women's desires and biases. "I'm thirty-four, but as a dater, I'm in my early twenties," he pointed out. A night owl, he studied the patterns of his female counterparts. "At 3 or 4 in the morning, you had very different characters," Andy said.

Late one night, he went online just as a novelist named Sandra from Brooklyn signed off. He wrote to her, asking for the name of her new novel. The title led him to Amazon, where he found her full name. Which led, of course, to Google, where he found an article about her from the UK *Guardian.* She'd written the novel in London while working for an "industrial espionage firm," composing the entire book as a PowerPoint presentation. Andy was understandably smitten with her creative theft of company time. Other work experience: She'd answered a newspaper ad by a professional gambler; she and three other women helped this seedy fellow cheat casinos at blackjack.

Intrigued, Andy felt pressure to come up with something interesting, so he asked her to accompany him on a tour of surveillance cameras in New York.

"A fine date choice," wrote Sandra, but she was now in L.A. visiting her family for a month, so that was probably that. Andy considered his options. He was headed to Vancouver soon anyway, and he did have a friend to stay with in L.A.

So he flew 3,000 miles for a lunch date. They arranged to meet at a Mexican restaurant "on the seedier end of Sunset Boulevard. Not seedy, really, just the end that wasn't totally posh and had some non-whites," Andy corrected himself. "Anyway, she was really cool, and her book is amazing, but we didn't have any chemistry."

They've kept in touch, as Andy generally does. Unlike the bulk of online daters crossing everyone they don't marry off a list, Andy doesn't banish people. He collects them. And so his international cabal of friends and comrades is always growing and cross-pollinating.

• • •

A few years later, Andy found me on Facebook. He'd started organizing political events, and thanked me for bringing him to his "first-ever march, demo-type thing." (One of those demo-type things even led him to his current long-term relationship.)

I asked Andy why he Facebook-posted so much about transplants, and he told me that three years earlier, his kidneys had failed abruptly. He'd spent hours a day with a dialysis tube drilled into his jugular vein. The news traveled through his network, and a friend stepped up to be a living donor.

On the day of the operation, Andy watched his friend wheeled unconscious past him, down one kidney, then went under himself. The liberated kidney was eased into the hole in Andy's front and woven into his blood vessels and digestive tubes.

The experience has changed his view of the world. It's even sunnier and more communitarian now. On the phone from London, Andy told me he could feel the love and goodwill pouring toward him in the hospital.

We touched on the topic of Sandra (Andy's "I flew 3,000 miles on my blind date" story), and he told me he's stayed in touch with her sporadically. "I believe the last thing she wrote," he told me, "is a book called *How Not To Write a Novel* with some bloke."

> He could feel the love and goodwill pouring toward him in the hospital.

"No way!" I shouted. "I know that bloke." His name is Howard, and we met years ago, on Nerve. Ever since, we've had a sporadic, mostly e-mail, friendship, with occasional long, commiserating phone calls about poverty and writing gigs. I hadn't talked to him in about a year, but he'd told me a lot about cowriting that book with his talented friend Sandy. So of course, I e-mailed Howard the Andy and Sandra story, and he wrote back to tell me that Sandy's second novel, *Cake*, includes the following passage:

"He said he had a friend who, when his marriage broke up, he'd left his job and traveled around the world playing the saxophone. He'd always played the saxophone, he played in a band—just a weekend band, this was in Bristol. Mark got a letter from him from Cuba, he was sitting in with Cuban bands and on his way to Zanzibar to some jazz festival."

As for Howard and Sandy? Their professional relationship, after four years, has become a romantic one as well.

Acknowledgments

Thanks to my editor Savannah Ashour, and to the brilliant cable TV show *Brooklyn vs. Bush,* where we met. Thanks also to my agent, Beth Vesel, and to Jim Smith, Cheryl Burke, Anne Elliott, Maria Luisa Tucker, Marcella Miller (a.k.a. Mom), Carolyn Weaver, Anthony Benedetto, Brad Polzin, and all the daters who generously shared their stories with me.